A Dictionary of
Muslim
Names

Presented to ....

....

From ....

Date ....

First published 2001
Reprinted 2010
© Goodword Books 2010

Goodword Books
1, Nizamuddin West Market, New Delhi-110 013
email: info@goodwordbooks.com
Printed in India

see our complete catalogue at

www.goodwordbooks.com
www.goodword.net

A Dictionary of
Muslim
Names

EDITED BY
PROF. S.A. RAHMAN

Goodword
B·O·O·K·S

Contents

Introduction

Young and inexperienced parents often give a name to their child without considering its meaning, correct pronunciation and spelling, or even its musicality. It is only once in a lifetime that a child can be named, therefore it is only fitting that all parents make a well-considered choice of appellation in terms of sense, sound and orthography. It is with this precise aim that this dictionary of names has been prepared.

Muslims all over the world have mostly preferred Arabic-Islamic names to names from Persian and other oriental languages like Turkish and Hebrew. In this selection, however, a good number of non-Arabic names have also been included, because of their present popularity with Muslims. We should stress here that the very best dictionaries have been consulted to elicit their most exquisite meanings. The majority listed in this selection as Turkish are actually Arabic, these having been passed on to us through Turkish written in Arabic script, e.g. Rifat رفعت, Nikhat نکهت, Hashmat حشمت, etc. These can otherwise be written with a *ta marboota* or the round *ta* ة as حشمة , نکهة , رفعة . This, however, is not in vogue. Certain names like Hiba هبة, Ama أمة, Ayesha عائشة , etc. have been written with ta marboota, because they have been directly passed on to us through the Arabic language, and generally apply to women. Some Hebrew examples have also been included, because they are the names of prophets.

In this compilation, mostly single-word names have been listed, e.g. Bashir, Basim, Fatima, etc. However, compound names can be made by prefixing, suffixing or inserting additional components. For example, Bashir can be used as part of a compound, as in Muhammad Bashir Ahmad, or Bashir Ahmad Kashif or Kashif Bashir Muhammad Ahmad. However, we should be careful in making composites of this kind, for, while Khalilullah, or Khalilur Rahman, meaning "the friend of Allah" are grammatically correct and appropriate in meaning, combinations such as Akhlaqur Rahman or Akhlaqullah, i.e. Allah's morals, may be unacceptable.

With the changing times, trends and needs are also changing. On application forms and in official documents, we are generally required to write a name consisting of three components, i.e. first name, middle name and last name. In this case, the first is generally that of the person concerned, while the middle one is his father's and the last is the name of his grandfather or of his family. To save future generations from difficulties and embarrassments, we too should fall in line with this development. However, this three-component name need not necessarily conform to the foregoing formula, in that the three parts or components may or may not refer, either individually or jointly, to parentage or the family. For example, Muhammad Ahmad Saleem, or Saleem Ahmad Khan, or Tameez Fatima Bano or Fatima Bano Khan, etc., can be names of individuals, without any of their components having familial connotations.

Typical Arabic sounds have been represented as they are ordinarily pronounced in English, Persian, Turkish or Urdu. For example the hard 'h' or the deep glottal 'a' have been written as 'h' and 'a' as in Hamidullah and Abdullah. Only the deep glottal 'k' has been transcribed as 'q'.

Though these Arabic-Persian-Islamic names are generally favoured by Muslims and Arabic-speaking Christians, there is an increasing trend among educated Indians, irrespective of their religious affinities, to choose mellifluous Arabic names, which have good meanings. The entries in this dictionary have been arranged in English alphabetical order to permit quick and easy reference for those who do not read Arabic script, but who would like, nevertheless, to give their children soft-sounding and meaningful names of Arabic, Persian or Turkish origin.

We do hope that this dictionary will serve as an excellent guide for responsible parents in their quest for appropriate and meaningful names for their children, of which the latter may feel proud when they come to know their significance.

I would like to thank my student, Shah Nawaz, for compiling an appendix of names of historical importance, such as those of the companions of the Prophet Muhammad, etc. This can be found at the end of the book.

S.A. Rahman
Jawahar Lal Nehru University
New Delhi

Male Names

A

Adam	آدم	name of the first man and Prophet of Allah; father of mankind
Alam	عالم	the world, the universe
Alamgir	عالمگیر	world conqueror
Aali	عالی	high, tall
Amir	عامر	prosperous, populous, civilised, full of life, large
Aqil	عاقل	wise, judicious, intelligent, prudent
Arif	عارف	learned, expert, authority, saint, the highest position a mystic can attain
Asif	آصف	name of a courtier in the kingdom of Prophet Sulaiman who is noted for his intelligence
Asir	آسر	captivating, fascinating
Abbad	عباد	worshipper
Aban	أبان	old Arabic name
Abbas	عباس	a furious lion that mauls its prey to pieces; name of the Prophet Muhammad's Uncle
Abbood	عبّود	devoted worshipper of Allah

Abd	عبد	servant, devotee, slave
Abdullah	عبد الله	servant of Allah, slave of Allah; name of Prophet Muhammad's father
Abid	عابد	worshipper, adorer, devout
Abidin	عابدين	pl. of Abid عابد i.e. worshippers. A popular name among Muslims
Abidullah	عابد الله	worshipper of Allah
Zaynul Abidin	زين العابدين	best of the worshippers (of Allah)
Abrar	أبرار	pl. of Birr بر , obedience, gift
Absar	أبصار	pl. of Basar بصر, vision, sight
Nur-ul-Absar	نور الابصار	light of vision
Abu Ayyub	ابو ايوب	A well-known Sahaabi who had received the honour of offering hospitality to the Prophet Muhammadﷺ when he migrated to Madinah
Abu Bakr	أبوبكر	father of the young camel. The first Caliph of Islam
Abul Fazl	ابو الفضل	endowed with bounty, grace
Abu Hanifa	أبو حنيفه	founder of the Hanafi school of thought/ Islamic law
Abu Talib	أبو طالب	Father of seeker; name of the Prophet Muhammad's uncle
Abyan	أبين	clearer, more distinct
Abyaz	أبيض	white, bright, brilliant

Abul Bashar	أبو البشر	father of mankind. An epithet of Adam who was also the first Prophet
Adham	أدهم	black
Adib/Adeeb	أديب	well-mannered, courteous, polished, man of letters
Adeel	عديل	coeval, match
Adil	عادل	just, upright, righteous
Adli	عدلى	pertaining to justice
Adnan	عدنان	A descendant of Ismail and traditional ancestor of the North Arabian tribes... who called themselves 'the sons of Adnan'
Affan	عفّان	modest; Father of Caliph Uthman عثمان
Afif	عفيف	chaste, modest, virtuous, honest, righteous, upright, decent
Afif-ud-Din	عفيف الدين	virtuous of the religion (Islam)
Afsar (Per.)	أفسر	crown
Afsar-ud-Din	أفسر الدين	adorning the religion (Islam)
Aftab (Per.)	آفتاب	sun
Aftab-ud-Din	آفتاب الدين	sun of the religion (Islam)
Afzaal	أفضال	kindness, grace, favours, virtues
Afzal	أفضل	better, superior, prominent
Aghlab	أغلب	superior, supreme
Ahad	أحد	one, unique, without partner; one of the names of Allah

Abd-ul-Ahad	عبد الاحد	servant of the only One (Allah)
Ahdaf	أهداف	pl. of هدف , aim, goal, target
Ahmad	أحمد	the most praised; one of the names of the Prophet Muhammadﷺ; I praise (First person present imperfect verb)
Ahmadullah	أحمد الله	I praise Allah
Ahsab	أحسب	nobler, more respected, of higher nobility
Ahsan	أحسن	better, superior
Ajawid	أجاويد	pl. of Jawwad جواد , open-handed, generous, noble
Ajmal	أجمل	more beautiful, extremely beautiful, handsome
Ajwad	أجود	better, more generous
Akbar	أكبر	greater, bigger, greatest, most pious, honourable
Akhlaq	أخلاق	good manners, morals
Akhtar (Per.)	أختر	star, good luck
Akhund	اخوند	honorific title of someone learned in religious matters
Akhund zada	اخوند زاده	son of a person learned in religious matters
Akif	عاكف	devoted to, dedicated to, persevering in, busily engaged, attached, intent
Akmal	أكمل	more complete, more perfect
Akram	أكرم	more generous, nobler, bountiful

Abul Alaa	ابو الاعلىٰ	father of glory
Ala-ud-Din	علاء الدين	glory of religion, excellence of religion (Islam)
Alam-ul-Huda	علم الهدىٰ	banner of guidance
Aleem	عليم	learned, expert, scholar, omniscient; one of the names of Allah
Aleemuddin	عليم الدين	A learned person in religion
Abdul Aleem	عبد العليم	servant of the All-knowing (Allah)
Ali	علی	high, lofty, sublime, eminent, excellence, noble, honourable; one of the names of Allah; fourth Caliph of Islam; name of the Prophet Muhammad's cousin & son-in-law
Abdul Ali	عبد العلی	servant of the most High
Allal	علّال	comforter
Almas	ألماس	diamond
Altaf	ألطاف	pl. of Lutf لطف , Kindness, grace, favour
Altaf Husain	ألطاف حسين	kindness of Husain
Aman	أمان	trust, safety, security, protection, tranquillity, peace of mind, calmness
Amanullah	أمان الله	trust, care of Allah, protection of Allah
Amanuddin	أمان الدين	trust of the religion (Islam)
Amani	أمانی	pl. of Umniya أمنية , wish, aspiration, hope
Ameer	أمير	chieftain, ruler, prince, commander, lord, leader, master

Amid	عميد	pillar, support, head
Amiduddawlah	عميد الدولة	support of the state, (It is used both as name & title)
Amin	أمين	trustworthy, faithful, reliable, custodian, honest
Al-Amin	الأمين	an epithet of the Prophet Muhammad ﷺ
Aminuddin	أمين الدين	trustworthy in religion (Islam)
Amjad	أمجد	most glorious, most distinguished, more illustrious, most venerable, most noble
Amjaad	أمجاد	pl. of majd مجد, glory, honour
Ammar	عمار	virtuous, pious, devout, religious, tolerant
Amr	عمرو	old Arabic name
Anan	عنان	clouds
Anas	أنس	friend
Anjum	انجم	plural of Najm نجم, stars
Aniq	أنيق	neat, elegant, smart
Anis	أنيس	friend, close companion, sociable, intimate friend, companion
Ansar	أنصار	pl. of Nasir ناصر, friend, patron, supporter
Ansari	أنصارى	relation through ancestry to an Ansar; the people who helped the Prophet when he migrated to Madinah
Antar	عنتر	hero in a story of chivalry
Anwar	أنوار	rays of light, lustre; pl. of Nur نور, light

Anwarulkarim	أنوارالكريم	lights of the Beneficent (Allah)
Anwar	أنور	more bright, more brilliant, more radiant, more luminous
Anwar-al-Sadat	أنور السادات	the most brilliant of the Sayyids
Aqdas	أقدس	most holy, more or most sacred
Aqeel	عقيل	insight, mind, intellect, judiciousness, wise, sensible man
Aqib	عاقب	successor, an epithet of the Prophet Muhammadﷺ
Aqmar	أقمر	bright, brilliant, luminous, moonlit
Aqqad	عقاد	maker of trimmings, haberdasher
Arafat	عرفات	a plain twelve miles south west of Makkah where pilgrims spend a day performing special worship of Allah during the Hajj
Areef	عريف	learned, expert, authority
Arib	أريب	wise, intelligent, bright, brilliant, clever
Arij	أريج	fragrant, sweet-smelling
Arkan	أركان	pl. of Rukn ركن, support, prop, pillar
Arqam	أرقم	writer, the best recorder; companion of the Prophet Muhammad ﷺ
Arshad	أرشد	most rightly guided, most reasonable
Arshaq	ارشق	handsome, more elegant, more graceful
Arwah	أروح	more delicate, more gracious
Arzu (Per.)	آرزو	wish, hope, love

As'ad	أسعد	virtuous, pious, happier, luckier
Asad	اسد	lion
Asadullah	اسد الله	lion of Allah. Title of Ali (R.A.)
Asghar	أصغر	younger, smaller, minute
Ali Asghar	على أصغر	infant son of Imam Husayn who attained martyrdom in the Karbala when he was a suckling baby
Ashab	أصهب	reddish, blond, fair
Ashfaq	أشفاق	pl. of Shafaqa شفقة, kindness, compassion, sympathy, pity, mercy, favours.
Ashiq	عاشق	adorer, lover, suitor
Ashiq Ali	عاشق على	adorer of Ali
Ashiq Muhammad	عاشق محمد	adorer of the Prophet Muhammadﷺ
Ashja	أشجع	more courageous, braver
Ashraf	أشرف	more honourable, most distinguished, eminent, more nobler
Asil	اصيل	of noble origin, highborn, pure, pristine
Asim	عاصم	protector, guardian, chaste, safe
Asir	أثير	preferred, noble, exquisite
Askari	عسكرى	soldier
Aslam	أسلم	very safe, safeguarded, better, more perfect, more complete
Asra	أسرىٰ	travel by night

Asrar	أسرار	secrets, mysteries, pl. of Sirr سرّ, secret
Ata	عطاء	gift, present, favour, bounty, generosity
Ataullah	عطاء الله	gift of Allah
AtaurRahman	عطاء الرحمٰن	gift of the merciful (Allah)
Athar	أطهر	purer, more virtuous, most pious, meticulously neat and clean
Atif	عاطف	compassionate, affectionate, sympathetic. kind-hearted, loving
Atiq	عتيق	ancient, noble, antiquated
Atir	عاطر	fragrant, aromatic
Attar	عطّار	perfumer, perfume vendor
Atuf	عطوف	affectionate, kind hearted, compassionate, loving
Atyab	اطيب	scrupulously clean, refined, most noble, excellent
Aurangzeb (Per)	اورنگزيب	ornament of the throne, a person befitting the throne
Awad	عوض	reward, compensation
Awn	عون	support, help
Awwab	اواب	sincere repentant, supplicant
Awwal	أول	first. Al-Awwalالاول, the first: one of the names of Allah
Ayaat	آيات	pl. of Ayatآية, sign, verse of the Qur'an
Ayat	آية	sign, revelation, verse of the Qur'an

Ayatullah	آية الله	sign of Allah
Ayman	أيمن	lucky, blessed, right-hand, right, on the right, fortunate
Ayn	عين	source
Aynul Hasan	عين الحسن	Hasan like. Hasan was the name of the Prophet Muhammad's grandson from his daughter Fatima
Aynul Hayat	عين الحياة	fountain of life
Ayyub	أيوب	a Prophet, the biblical Job
Azad (Per)	آزاد	free, liberated
Azam	أعظم	greater, greatest, more important, most important, most pious, most exalted
Azfar	أظفر	most victorious, winner
Azmat	عظمة	majesty, pride, grandeur, greatness
Azhaar	أزهار	pl. of Zahra زهرة, flower, blossom
Azhar	أزهر	more glittering, blooming, shining, bright, brilliant, luminous, radiant
Azhar	اظهر	more evident, most apparent, most illuminated
Azim	عظيم	mighty, magnificent, glorious, great, dignified, exalted, determined; one of the names of Allah
Abdul Azim	عبد العظيم	servant of the Mighty (Allah)
Aziz	عزيز	mighty, strong, illustious, highly esteemed, dearly loved, one of the names of Allah

Azizullah	عزيز الله	dear to Allah
Abdul Aziz	عبد العزيز	servant of the Almighty
Azmi	عزمىّ	one who fulfils his promise
Azraf	أظرف	more elegant, more graceful; more humorous
Azud	عضد	upper arm, stength, power, support
Azududdin	عضد الدين	support of religion (Islam)
Azzam	عزّام	very determined, resolved, resolute

B

Baadi	البادى	distinct, evident, plain, clear
Baahi	الباهى	glorious, magnificent
Baaligh	بالغ	major
Baari	بارئ	originator, creator
Abdul Baari	عبد البارى	servant of the Creator
Lutf-ul-Baari	لطف البارى	kindness of the Creator
Sayful Baari	سيف البارى	sword of the Creator
Baari'	بارع	brilliant, superior, outstanding
Baariq	بارق	shining, lightning, bright, illuminating
Babar	ببر	tiger
Badi'	بديع	wonderful, marvellous, unique, amazing

Badiul Alam	بديع العالم	unique in the world
Badiuz Zaman	بديع الزمان	genius of the time
Badr	بدر	full moon
Badr-e-Alam	بدر عالم	full moon of the world
Badruddin	بدرالدين	full moon of religion (Islam)
Badrud Duja	بدرالدجیٰ	full moon of the dark
Baha	بهاء	beauty, glow, splendour, magnificence
Bahauddin	بهاء الدين	glow of the religion (Islam)
Bahir	باهر	dazzling, brilliant
Bahi	بهی	splendid, brilliant, shining.
Bahiyud Din	بهیّ الدين	radiant, brilliant of the religion (Islam)
Bahjat	بهجات	splendours, pl. of Bahjah بهجة, delight, joy
Bakhit (Per)	بخيت	lucky, fortunate
Bakhsh (Per)	بخش	gift, fortunate, give, forgive
Allah Bakhsh (Ar. Per.)	الله بخش	gift of Allah
Ilahi Bakhsh (Ar. Per.)	الهی بخش	gift of Allah
Khuda Bakhsh (Ar. Per.)	خدا بخش	gift of Khuda (Allah)
Taaj Bakhsh	تاج بخش	King maker

Bakht (Per.)	بخت	luck, fortune
Bakhtiyar (Per)	بختيار	fortunate, lucky
Bakur	بكور	precocious, early coming
Baligh	بليغ	eloquent, learned, one who is qualified in the art of speech
Baqa	بقاء	survival, immortality, eternity
Baqi	باقى	permanent, everlasting, eternal
Abdul Baqi	عبد الباقى	servant of the Everlasting (Allah)
Baqir	باقر	fierce lion, abounding in knowledge, erudite, learned
Barakat	بركات	blessings, good fortunes prosperities; pl. of Barakah بركة
Abul Barakat	ابو البركات	father of blessings, blissful.
Barakatullah	بركات الله	(barakat Allah) blessings of Allah
Bareeq	بريق	glitter, flash, lustre, brightness, brilliance, radiance
Barr	برّ	pious, upright, just; sing. of Abraar أبرار
Abdul Barr	عبد البر	servant of the All-benign
Barraq	برّاق	flashing, bright, brilliant, glittering
Bashar	بشر	man, mankind
Abul Bashar	ابو البشر	father of mankind
Khairul Bashar	خير البشر	the greatest man. An epithet of the Prophet Muhammadﷺ

Basharat	بشارت	good news, glad tidings
Bashir	بشير	harbinger, bringer of good news
Bashshar	بشار	herald, bringer of glad tidings
Basil	باسل	brave, bold, valiant
Basim	باسم	smiling
Baseem	بسيم	smiling
Baseer	بصير	sagacious, endowed with insight, wise; one of the names of Allah.
Abdul Basir	عبد البصير	servant of All-sagacious i.e. Allah
Basit	باسط	one who stretches, enlarges
Abdul Basit	عبد الباسط	servant of the Expander i.e. Allah
Bassam	بسّام	smiling
Batal	بطل	brave, champion, hero.
Batin	باطن	inward, within, secret, esoteric; one of the names of Allah
Abdul Batin	عبد الباطن	servant of the Inward
Baz	باز	falcon
Bazlur Rahman	بذل الرحمن	generosity of the All-merciful
Bedar (Per)	بيدار	wakeful, attentive, enlightened
Bedaruddin	بيدار الدين	attentive to the religion (Islam)
Beg	بك	honorific title i.e. lord
Bilal	بلال	water, moisture, freshness, river, sea. A

		sahaabi i.e. the companion of the Prophet Muhammadﷺ who was also the first muazzin in Islam
Binyamin (Heb)	بن يامين	name of the brother of Prophet Yusuf
Bishr	بشر	joy, happiness, cheerfulness
Bukhari	بخارى	Muhammad ibn Ismail al-Bukhari (810-70) author of one of the Sahih Hadith i.e. collection of the Prophet Muhammad's traditions
Bulbul	بلبل	nightingale
Burhan	برهان	proof, evidence
Al-Burhan	البرهان	the proof
Burhan-ud-Din	برهان الدين	proof of the religion (Islam)

D

Dabir	دابر	root, origin, ultimate, bygone
Daiyan	ديّان	a mighty ruler, judge, guard, protector
Dalil	دليل	guide, model, leader, example
Dana (Per)	دانا	wise, learned
Daniyal (Heb)	دانيال	a Prophet of Allah
Dara (Per)	دارا	possessor, sovereign
Darvesh	درويش	holy man
Dastgir (Per)	دستگير	protector, saint

Dawud	داؤد	a Prophet and father of Prophet Sulaiman in the Bible, he is known as David
Abu Dawud	ابوداؤد	author of one of the Sahih Hadith (d.875)
Didar (Per)	دیدار	vision, sight
Dil (Per)	دل	heart, mind
Dil Nwaz (Per)	دلنواز	soothing heart, mind
Dil-awar (Per)	دلاور	bold, brave
Dilwar (Per)	دلوار	bold, courageous
Din	دین	religion, faith, belief
Saifuddin	سیف الدین	sword of the religion
Diwan	دیوان	royal court, tribunal of justice

Diwan Muhammadدیوان محمد court of the Prophet Muhammdﷺ

Dost Muhammadدوست محمد friend of the Prophet Muhammadﷺ

| Dost (Per) | دوست | friend |
| Duha/Zuha | ضحی | forenoon. (This name is generally pronounced as Zohya in non-Arabic speaking countries like India/ Pakistan) |

E

Ebrahim (Heb) =Ibrahimابرهیم name of one Prophet

Ehsan =Ihsan إحسان favour, good

Ehtesham =Ihtisham احتشام modesty, decency

Ejaz =Ijaz	اعجاز	miracle, wondorous nature
Elias (Heb)=Ilyas	إلياس	name of one Prophet
Emad =Imad	عماد	pillar
Emir =Ameer	أمير	prince, leader, head
Enam =Inam	إنعام	award, favour, gift
Enayat =Inayat	عنايت	attention, favore, care

F

Faiz	فائز	victorious, triumphant, successful
Al-Faiz	الفائز	name of a Fatimid Caliph
Farih	فارح	happy
Fadi	فادى	redeemer
Fahd	فهد	leopard, lynx
Faheem	فهيم	intelligent, judicious, learned, erudite
Fahmi	فهمى	intelligent, intellectual
Faid	فائد/فايد	benefit, advantage, gain, worth, welfare
Faiq	فائق	excellent, outstanding, distinguished, superior
Fajr	فجر	dawn, rise, beginning, start
Fikhar	فخار	honour, pride, glory
Fakhir	فاخر	excellent, superior, magnificent, honourable, precious, proud

Fakhr	فخر	glory, pride, honour
Fakhr-ud-Din	فخر الدين	Pride of the religion (Islam)
Fakhr-ud-Dawlah	فخر الدوله	glory of the kingdom/state
Fakhri	فخرى	proud (for noble cause), honorary
Falah	فلاح	success, prosperity
Falih	فالح	fortunate, lucky, successful, prosperous
Faqih	فقيه	jurist, scholar in fiqh (Islamic jurisprudence)
Faqir	فقير	poor, needy, one renounces the world i.e. Sufi mendicant
Farah	فرح	happiness, delight
Abul Farah	ابو الفرح	father of joy i.e. happy, glad
Faraj	فرَج	comfort, relief, ease, repose
Abul Faraj	ابو الفرج	possessor of comfort, father of comfort, comfortable
Farman	فرمان	order, decree
Farmanullah	فرمان الله	(*faraman allah*) order of Allah
Farhan	فرحان	glad, happy, joyful, cheerful, delighted
Farahat	فرحات	joys, delights
Fari	فارع	tall, towering, lofty
Farid	فريد	unique, matchless, precious
Fariduddin	فريد الدين	unique of the religion (Islam)

Farih	فرح	happy, delight
Faris	فارس	horseman, knight
Farrukh (Per)	فرخ	beautiful-faced, happy, auspicious, fortunate
Farooq	فاروق	one who distinguishes truth from falsehood and right from wrong, just. Title of the Caliph Umar
Fasih	فصيح	eloquent, fluent, well-spoken
Fasih-ur-Rahman فصيح الرحمٰن		(Faseeh al-Rahman): eloquent (by grace of Rahman i.e. Allah)
Fatih	فاتح	one who eases difficulties, conquerer
Fath	فتح	victory, conquest, triumph, success
Abul Fath	أبو الفتح	father of victory, victorious
Fathullah	فتح الله	victory granted by Allah, victory of Allah
Fathi	فتحى	one who wins victory after victory
Fatin	فاتن	clever, fascinating
Fatin	فطن، فطين	intelligent, sagacious, smart, clever
Fattah	فتاح	conqueror, victor, one who opens, one who eases difficulties; an attribute of Allah
Abdul Fattah	عبد الفتاح	('abd al-Fattah) servant of the conqueror i.e. Allah
Fattan	فتان	charming, bright
Fattooh	فتوح	the little conqueror, diminutive of Fattah
Fawwaz	فواز	winner of victory after victory, successful

Fawz	فوز	victory, triumph, success
Fawzy	فوزی	triumphant, victorious, successful
Faisal	فیصل	umpire, arbitrator, decisive, sword, a judge
Fayyaz	فیاض	generous, munificent, most bountiful, most generous
Faiz	فیض	super abundance, effluence, plenty, generosity, grace, favour, bounty
Faizullah	فیض الله	abundance from Allah
Faizul Anwar	فیض الانوار	abundance of light or graces
Faizuddin	فیض الدین	bounty of religion (Islam)
Fayzul Haq	فیض الحق	grace of the Truth i.e. Allah
Faiz-e-Rabbaani	فیض ربانی	possessing divine surplus
Faizi	فیضی	endowed with superabundance
Fazil	فاضل	an accomplished person, knowledgeable virtuous, superior, outstanding, eminent
Fazl	فضل	favour, grace, kindness, gift, present, bounty, excellence, virtue, extra
Abul Fazl	ابو الفضل	see Abu
Fazle Ilahi	فضل الهی	bounty of Allah
Fazlullah	فضل الله	bounty of Allah
Fazlul Haq	فضل الحق	bounty of the Truth i.e. Allah
Fazle Rabbi	فضل ربی	bounty of my Lord
Fazli	فضلی	kind, bountiful, graceful, virtuous

Fida	فداء	sacrifice, redemption
Firas	فراس	perspicacity
Firasah	فراسة	perspicacity, acumen
Fairoz/Firoz	فيروز	turquoise
Fuad	فؤاد	the heart
Furoogh (Per)	فروغ	splendour, light, brightness
Furookh	فروخ	sprout, shoot, young (bird)
Furqan	فرقان	criterion (between right and wrong), proof, evidence. another name for the Qur'an
Futuh	فتوح	victories, conquests; pl. of فتح
Fuzail	فضيل	diminutive of Fazl

G

Gauhar (Per)	گوهر	gem, jewel, noble
Ghaffar	غفار	most forgiving, one of the names of Allah
Abdul Ghaffar	عبد الغفار	servant of the All-forgiving
Ghafur	غفور	most forgiving
Abdul Ghafur	عبد الغفور	servant of the All-forgiving
Ghais	غيث	rain
Ghaiyyas	غيّاث	helper, reliever, winner
Ghalib	غالب	conqueror, victor, winner, dominator

Ghallab	غلاب	ever victorious, triumphant
Ghani	غنيّ	rich, wealthy, prosperous, all-sufficient, one of the names of Allah
Abdul Ghani	عبد الغنى	('abd al-ghani): servant of the All-sufficient
Ghanim	غانم	successful
Gharib	غريب	poor, needy, humble; stranger
Ghassan	غسّان	prime, vigour (of youth)
Ghaus	غوث	help, aid, rescue, succour
Ghazanfar	غضنفر	lion, title of Caliph Ali
Ghazi	غازى	conqueror, hero, gallant soldier
Ghiyas	غياث	deliverance from hardships, succorer, aid given in time of need, rain
Ghiyas-ud-Din	غياث الدين	helper of the religion (Islam)
Ghofran	غفران	pardon, forgiveness
Ghulam	غلام	servant, boy, youth

H

Habab	حباب	aim, goal, end
Haafiz	حافظ	title of a man who has memorised the whole Quran; guardian, protector, attribute of Allah
Abdul Haafiz	عبد الحافظ	servant of the Guardian i.e. Allah

Hakim	حاكم	judge, ruler, governor, leader, chief
Abdul Hakim	عبد الحاكم	servant of the Judge
Hamid	حامد	praiser (of Allah)
Haris	حارس	vigilant, guardian, protector
Haris	حارث	ploughman, cultivator, agnomen of lion
Hashim	هاشم	great-grandfather of the Prophet Muhammadﷺ
Hashimi	هاشمى	Hashmite, a nisba (relation) through ancestry to the Banu Haashim
Habib	حبيب	beloved, dear, friend
Habibullah	حبيب الله	friend of Allah, dear to Allah
Hadaya	هدايا	gifts, presents, pl. of Hadiyya
Hadi	هادى	one who leads to the right path, guide, one of the names of Allah
Abdul Hadi	عبد الهادى	servant of the Guide (Allah)
Hafiz	حفيظ	guardian, protector
Abdul Hafiz	عبد الحفيظ	servant of the Guardian (Allah)
Hafs	حفص	collecting, gathering
Haidar	حيدر	lion. Title of Caliph Ali
Haji	حاجّ	title of someone who has performed *Hajj*
Hakam	حكم	arbitrator, judge
Abdul Hakam	عبد الحكم	servant of the Arbitrator

Hakeem	حكيم	wise, sage, judicious, prudent
Abdul Hakeem	عبد الحكيم	servant of the All-wise i.e. Allah
Halif	حليف	ally
Halim	حليم	patient, tolerant, clement
Abdul Halim	عبد الحليم	servant of the All-clement i.e. Allah
Hamas	حمس	enthusiasm, fervour
Hamd	حمد	praise, laudation of Allah
Hamid	حميد	all-laudable
Abdul Hamid	عبد الحميد	servant of the All-laudable
Hamidullah	حميد الله	praised by Allah
Hamim	حميم	close friend
Hammad	حماد	praising (Allah)
Hammam	همّام	energetic, active
Hammud	حمّود	much praise to Allah
Hamud	حمود	praised, commended, praiseworthy, commendable
Hamza	حمزة	lion. Name of the Prophet Muhammad's uncle.
Hani	هانئ	joyful, happy
Hanif	حنيف	true believer, true faith, upright
Hanifud Din	حنيف الدين	true of religion (Islam)
Hanin	حنين	yearning, desire

Hannan	حنّان	compassionate, merciful, affectionate, tender-hearted
Hanoon	حنون	compassionate, merciful, affectionate, tender-hearted, soft hearted
Haq	حقّ	true, truth, real, right, just
Abdul Haq	عبد الحق	servant of the Truth i.e. Allah
Haqqani	حقّانى	correct, right, proper
Haqqi	حقّى	a person who upholds the truth, just
Hariz	حريز	strong, secure, guarded
Haroon	هارون	chief, protector, guard, the wealth of the entire universe, a Prophet known as Aaron in the Bible and brother of Prophet Moses
Harun-al-Rashid	هارون الرشيد	Celebrated Abbasid Caliph (786-809)
Hasan	حسن	handsome, beautiful, good-looking
Abul Hasan	أبو الحسن	father of Hasan
Hasanat	حسنات	good deeds, kind acts, favours
Hasnain	حسنين	the two Hasans, Hasan and Husain, the two sons of Caliph Ali and it is used as name of one person
Hashmat	حشمت	pomp, magnificence
Hasher	حاشر	collector
Hashim	هاشم	one who smashes or breaks anything to pieces. Grandfather of the Prophet Muhammadﷺ

Hasib	حسيب	noble, respected, highborn, esteemed
Abdul Hasib	عبد الحسيب	('abd-al-Haseeb) servant of the Reckoner
Hasif	حصيف	judicious, wise, prudent, sagacious
Hasim	حاسم	decisive, definite
Hasin	حسين	handsome
Hasin	حصين	strong, secure, immune
Hassan	حسّان	very handsome, beautifier
Hatem	حاتم	judge, justice, decider
Hatif	هاتف	praiser; a voice from heaven, or from an invisible speaker; guardian angel
Hayat	حيات	life
Haydar	حيدر	see Haidar
Haysam	هيثم	loin
Hayy	حىّ	alive, living
Hayyan	حيّان	lively, energetic
Abdul Hayy	عبد الحىّ	servant of the Living i.e. Allah
Hazrat	حضرت	an honorific title, used at the beginning of a name
Hazim	حازم	firm, resolute, energetic, judicious, discreet, prudent
Hiba	هبة	gift
Hibatullah	هبة الله	gift of Allah

Hidayatullah	هدايت الله	guidance of Allah
Hidayat-ul-haq	هدايتالحق	(hidaayat al-haqq) guidance of the Truth i.e. Allah
Hikmat	حكمت	wisdom
Hilal	هلال	crescent, new moon
Hilali	هلالى	crescent-like
Hilmi	حلمى	patient, tolerant, lenient, clement, wise
Himayat	حمايت	protection, safeguarding, sheltering
Himmat	همت	ambition, endeavour, resolution, determination
Hisham	هشام	beneficence, generosity. Name of a *sahabi*
Hud	هود	a Prophet title of the 11th sura of the Quran
Huda	هدىٰ	right, guidance, right path
Nurul Huda	نور الهدىٰ	light of the right guidance (of Allah)
Hulayl	حليل	old Arabic name
Humam	همام	brave and noble, magnanimous, courageous, generous
Humamuddin	همام الدين	brave (person) of the religion (Islam), generous
Humayd	حميد	diminutive of Ahamd أحمد, praised
Humayun	همايون	auspicious, fortunate. Mohammad Humayun (d. 1556): name of a Mughal Emperor

Hurayra	هريرة	kitten. This name is usully used in combination with the word 'abu', as Abu-Hurayra
Husam	حسام	sword
Husamuddawlah	حسام الدوله	sword of the state
Husamuddin	حسام الدين	sword of religion (Islam)
Husayn	حسين	diminutive of Hasan حسن, beautiful. Imam Husayn: second son of Caliph Ali
Abul Husayn	ابو الحسين	father of Husayn: Caliph Ali
Husayni	حسينى	of Husayn; nisba (relation) through ancestry to Husayn
Husni	حسنى	(husnii): possessing beauty
Huzaifa	حذيفة	an old Arabic name, short-statured

I

Ibn	ابن	son
Isa	عيسى	a Prophet (Jesus)
Ibn Sina	ابن سينا	Sina was the father of Abu Ali ibn Sina, the celebrated physician Avicenna
Ibrahim (Heb)	ابراهيم	kind father, (combination of Abu أب, father and Rahim رحيم, kind) a Prophet's name
Ibtisam	ابتسام	smiling, smile

Idrak	إدارك	intellect, perception, achievement, attainment
Idris	إدريس	a Prophet, the biblical Enoch/Henoch
Iftikhar	افتخار	honour, grace, glory, pride, repute
Iftikhar-ud-Din	افتخار الدين	pride of the religion (Islam)
Ihsan	احسان	benevolence, charity, sincerity, beneficence, kindness, kind act, performance of good deeds
Ihsanul Haq	احسان الحق	kindness of the Truth i.e. Allah
Ihtisham	احتشام	chastity, modesty, decency, decorum
Ijaz	اعجاز	miracle, inimitability, astonishment, wondrous nature
Ijazul Haq	اعجاز الحق	inimitability of the Truth i. e. Allah
Ijlal	إجلال	glorification, exaltation, honesty, integrity, fidelity, faithfulness
Ikhlas	اخلاص	sincerity, purity
Ikhtiyar	اختيار	choice, preference, selection
Iklil	إكليل	crown, garland
Ikrima	عكرمة	a female pigeon. Name of an illustrious *sahabi*
Ikram	إكرام	honouring, glory, esteem, respect, veneration
Ikramullah	إكرام الله	glory of Allah
Ikramul Haqq	إكرام الحق	glory of the Truth i.e. Allah

Iksir	إكسير	elixir
Ilahi	إلهى	my lord (for Allah), divine
Ilham	إلهام	inspiration, revelation
Ilias (Heb)	إلياس	see Ilyas
Ilyas (Heb)	إلياس	a Prophet, the biblical Elias
Imad	عماد	pillar, post, support
Imaduddin	عماد الدين	pillar of the faith (Islam)
Imam	إمام	one who leads communal prayer, leader, chief
Iman	إيمان	belief, faith in Allah
Imdad	امداد	help, aid, support
Imran	عمران	population, civilization, careful observance of rules of etiquette. Father of Maryam (mother of Prophet 'Isa) i.e Mary, mother of Jesus
Imtiaz	امتياز	distinction, privilege, mark of honour
Inam	إنعام	gift, present, prize, grant, reward
Inamul Haq	إنعام الحق	gift of the Truth i.e. Allah
Inayat	عنايت	care, concern, favour, bounty, kindness
Inayatullah	عنايت الله	care of Allah
Inayatur Rahman	عنايت الرحمن	care of the most Gracious i.e. Allah
Inayatuddin	عنايت الدين	care of religion (Islam)
Insaf	إنصاف	justice, impartiality, fairness, equity

Inshirah	انشراح	delight, happiness, cheerfulness
Intisar	انتصار	victory, triumph
Iqbal	اقبال	prosperity, good fortune, good-luck, responsiveness, welfare
Irfan	عرفان	knowledge, learning, perception, erudition, discernment, science, wisdom, knowledge
Irshad	إرشاد	guidance, guiding/hand, instruction
Irtida	ارتضاء	see Irtiza
Irtiza	ارتضاء	contentment, approval
Irtiza Husain	ارتضاء حسين	approval of Husayn
Isa	عيسى	a Prophet, the biblical Jesus
Abu Isa	أبو عيسى	father of Isa
Isad	إسعاد	making happy or prosperous, blessing, favoring
Isam	عصام	self-made
Ishaq (Heb)	اسحاق	one who laughs. A Prophet, the biblical Isaac and son of Prophet Ibrahim
Ishfaq	إشفاق	compassion, sympathy, pity
Ishtiyaq	اشتياق	fondness, wish, desire, yearning, eagerness
Iskandar	اسكندر	name of a Greek king, Alexander. Iskander Mirza: President of Pakistan (1956-58)
Islah	إصلاح	reform, improvement, betterment
Islam	اسلام	to bow ones head in submission, surrender (to the will of Allah) name of the religion of the Muslims

Ismail (Heb)	إسماعيل	a Prophet, the biblical Ishmael and son of Prophet Ibrahim
Ismat	عصمت	purity, chastity, modesty
Isra	إسراء	travel by night
Israr	إسرار	secret, mystery
Israil	اسرائيل	another name of Prophet Ya'qub علیه السلام
Istifa'	اصطفاء	to choose, to prefer, to give prefer to one over the other
Itidal	إعتدال	moderation, moderateness, clemency
Itimad	إعتماد	reliance, dependence, confidence
Iyad	إياد	support, might, strength
Izaz	إعزاز	honour, esteem, regard, affection, to respect an honour, or raise to an exalted position
Izazuddawlah	إعزازالدولة	honour of the state
Izz	عزّ	power, might, honour
Izzuddin	عزّالدين	honour of the religion (Islam)
Izzat	عزة	honour, fame, power

J

| Jabbar | جبار | powerful, mighty |
| Jabir | جابر | consoler, restorer, comforter |

Abdul Jabbar	عبدالجبار	servant of the All-compeller/the Omnipotent i.e. Allah
Jadwal	جدول	brook, rivulet
Jafar	جعفر	spring, rivulet
Jah	جاه	rank
Jahan (Per)	جهان	world
Shah Jahan (Per)	شاه جهان	king of the world
Jahangir (Per)	جهانگیر	world conqueror
Jahid	جاهد	diligent, hardworking, striving
Jalal	جلال	majesty, grandeur, glory
Jalal-ud-Din	جلال الدین	the majesty of religion (Islam)
Jalil	جلیل	great, exalted, magnificent
Abdul Jalil	عبد الجلیل	servant of the Exalted i.e. Allah
Jamal	جمال	beauty, grace
Jamal-ud-Din	جمال الدین	beauty of the religion (Islam)
Jami	جامع	gatherer, collector, author, writer
Jamil	جمیل	handsome, attractive, impressive
Abdul Jamil	عبد الجمیل	servant of the Beautiful (attributed to Allah)
Jamuh	جموح	defiant
Jamshed (Per)	جمشید	the sun in Pisces
Jan (Per)	جان	life, sing

Jan-e-Alam	جان عالم	life of the world
Jan Muhammad	جان محمد	life of Muhammad
Jnab	جناب	an honorific title, Your Excellency
Jarullah	جار الله	neighbour of Allah
Jasim	جسيم	great and famous
Jasim-ud-Din	جسيم الدين	great (man) of the religion (Islam)
Jasir	جاسر	brave, bold, courageous, valiant
Jasur	جسور	brave, bold, courageous, valiant
Javed (Per)	جاويد	eternal, perpetual
Jawad	جواد	generous, liberal, open-handed
Jawahir	جواهر	jewels; pl. of Jawhar جوهر, jewel
Jawhar	جوهر	jewel, gem, essence
Jihad	جهاد	strive, holy war
Junayd	جنيد	diminutive of jund جند, army, soldiers

K

Kab	كعب	fame, honour, high rank
Kbir	كبير	great, grand, magnificent, senior, Allah's epithet
Kafi	كافى	sufficient, Al-Kafiالكافى, one of the names of Allah
Abdul Kafi	عبد الكافى	servant of the All-sufficient i.e. Allah

Kafil	كفيل	guarantor, surety, sponsor, responsible
Kalam	كلام	speech, conversation
Abul Kalam	ابوالكلام	father of speech, eloquent
Kalim	كليم	interlocutor, speaker, one of the two conversators
Kalimullah	كليم الله	one who conversed with Allah. An epithet of Prophet Moses
Kamal	كمال	perfection, completion, integrity
Kamaluddin	كمال الدين	perfection of religion (Islam)
Mustafa Kamal مصطفى كمال		founder of modern Turkey (1881-1938)
Kamil	كامل	perfect, complete, genuine, total, learned
Kamran (Per)	كامران	lucky, happy, success
Karam	كرم	generosity, bounty
Karamullah	كرم الله	bounty of Allah
Karamat	كرامت	act of generosity, magnificence, nobility, excellence
Kardar (Per)	كاردار	prime minister
Krim	كريم	kind, generous, benevolent, noble, bountiful, magnificent, gracious, merciful, an epithet of Allah
Abdul Karim	عبد الكريم	servant of the most generous i.e. Allah
Kashif	كاشف	discoverer
Kasib	كسيب	winner, provider

Kasir	كثير	much abundant, plenty
Kausar	كوثر	abundance, name of a river in Paradise.
Kaukab	كوكب	planet
Kaykaus (Per)	كيكاؤس	just, noble. King of Iran (d. 1058)
Kazim	كاظم	one who controls or suppresses his anger
Khaliq	خالق	creator
Abdul Khaliq	عبد الخالق	servant of the Creator i.e. Allah
Khatib	خاطب	suitor, matchmaker
Khabir	خبير	learned, expert, authority
Khadim	خادم	sevant
Khalaf	خلف	successor, heir
Khaldun	خلدون	name of a famous Muslim philosopher, historian & social scientist
Khalaf Hasan	خلف حسن	successor of Hasan
Khalid	خالد	immortal, eternal
Khalid ibn al-Walid	خالد ابن وليد	general to whom the Prophet Muhammadﷺ awarded the title of honour, Sword of Allah (d. 642)
Khalifa	خليفه	successor, viceroy, caliph, viceregent
Khalil	خليل	friend
Khalilullah	خليل الله	friend of Allah, an epithet of Prophet Ibrahimعليه السلام
Khaliq	خليق	qualified, suitable, worthy of

Khaliquz Zaman خليق الزمان		the qualified (person) of the era
Khaliqus Subhan خليق السبحان		worthy of the Glory (Allah)
Khalis	خالص	pure, true, clear, real
Khashi	خاشع	pious, devout
Khasib	خصيب	fruitful, prolific
Khatib	خطيب	orator, title of someone who delivers speech
Khatir	خاطر	heart, idea
Khair	خير	good, blessing, boon, wealth, benevolent, fortune
Abul Khair	أبو الخير	father of good work, virtuous
Khairuddin	خير الدين	boon of religion (Islam)
Khairul Bashar	خير البشر	best of mankind, an epithet of the Prophet Muhammadﷺ
Khairat	خيرات	blessings, good work, good deeds
Khayri	خيرىّ	benevolent, charitable, beneficent
Khayyam	خيّام	tent-maker
Khayyir	خيّرٌ	generous
Khazin	خازن	treasurer
Khizar	خضر	name of a Prophet
Khulud	خلود	immortality, eternity
Khurram (Per)	خرم	cheerful, glad, fresh
Khurshid (Per)	خورشيد	sun

Khuzayma	خزيمة	old Arabic name
Kibria	كبرياء	divine majesty, divine grandeur
Kifah	كفاح	struggle, fight
Kifayat	كفايت	self-sufficiency
Kohinoor (Per)	كوه نور	the mountain of light, name of a precious stone

L

Labib	لبيب	intelligent, reasonable, rational, wise
Layeeq	لئيق	worthy, capable, clever, sensible
Laiq	لائق	worthy, deserving, capable, decent
Lashkar (Per)	لشكر	soldier, army
Latif	لطيف	kind, gracious, courteous, gentle, friendly
Abdul Latif	عبد اللطيف	servant of the All-gentle i.e. Allah
Layyin	لين	tender, resilient
Liaqat	لياقت	decorum, decency, competence, worth, capability, merit
Lisan	لسان	tongue, language
Lisanuddin	لسان الدين	language of religion (Islam)
Luqman	لقمان	the sage Luqman...is the type of perfect wisdom, Lokman
Lut	لوط	Name of a great Prophet of Allah

Lutf	لطف	kindness, friendliness, gentleness, grace, courtesy, favour (from Allah)
Lutfullah	لطف الله	kindness of Allah, favour of Allah
Lutf-ur-Rahman	لطف الرحمن	favour of the All-merciful i.e. Allah
Lutfi	لطفى	kind, friendly, courteous

M

Majid	ماجد	glorious, noble, honourable, generous, Allah's attribute
Abdul Maajid	عبد الماجد	servant of the All-glorious i.e. Allah
Malik	مالك	owner, proprietor, master, lord. Allah's epithet
Abdul Maalik	عبد المالك	servant of the Owner i.e. Allah
Maali	معالى	noble, sublime, excellency
Mabruk	مبروك	blessed, prosperous
Madani	مدنى	urbane, civilized
Maad	معد	a old Arabian Tribes's name
Madih	مديح	praised, commendable
Mahasin	محاسن	pl. of Mahsana محسنة, beauty, attraction, virtue, merit
Abul Mahasin	ابو المحاسن	father of virtues, merits
Mahbub	محبوب	dear, beloved

Mahbubullah	محبوب الله	beloved of Allah
Mahdi	مهديّ	rightly guided
Mahfuz	محفوظ	safeguarded, well-protected, preserved, secure
Mahib	مهيب	majestic, dignified, magnificent
Mahir	ماهر	skilled, skilful, proficient
Mahjub	محجوب	hidden, covered, screened
Mahmood	محمود	praised, commendable, praiseworthy, lauded, laudable, elegant, attribute of the Prophet Muhammadﷺ
Mahrus	محروس	guarded, protected, secured
Mahzuz	محظوظ	fortunate
Mahtab (Per)	مهتاب	moon, moonlight
Maimun	ميمون	auspicious, prosperous, lucky, good fortunate, blessed
Maein	معين	fountain, spring
Maisara	ميسرة	ease, comfort
Maisur	ميسور	easy, successful, fortunate, lucky, prosperous
Majd	مجد	glory, honour, nobility
Majduddin	مجد الدين	the glory of the religion (Islam)
Majdi	مجدى	glorious, praiseworthy
Majeed	مجيد	glorious, noble, exalted, an epithet of Allah

Abdul Majeed	عبد المجيد	servant of the All-glorious i.e. Allah
Makhdoom	مخدوم	one who is held in reverence and served by others, lord, master
Makin	مكين	strong, firm
Makram	مكرم	noble trait, excellent quality
Malih	مليح	handsome
Maleek	مليك	reigning, ruling
Malik	ملك	an attribute of Allah, king, sovereign
Abdul Malik	عبد الملك	servant of the King i.e. Allah
Maluf	مألوف	familiar, popular
Mamdooh	ممدوح	praised, celebrated, famous, commended, laudable
Mamoon	مأمون	trustworthy honest, faithful, reliable, something about which one feels secure
Al-Mamoon	المأمون	seventh Abbasid caliph (813-33)
Manaf	(عبد) مناف	Abd Manaaf: an ancestor of the Prophet Muhammadﷺ
Man	معن	benefit
Manal	منال	attainment, acquisition, reachable
Manhal	منهل	fountain, spring of salubrious water
Mannan	منان	benevolent, bountiful, generous
Mansoor	منصور	assisted, aided (by God), victorious, triumphant

Mansooruddin	منصور الدين	victorious in religion (Islam)
Manus	مأنوس	friendly, sociable, polite
Manzoor	منظور	visible, perspective
Maqbool	مقبول	accepted, admitted, granted, approved
Maqsood	مقصود	intended, aimed at, object
Maram	مرام	wish, desire, aspiration
Maroof	معروف	favour, kindness, kind act, famous, noted
Marghoob	مرغوب	desired, desirable, pleasant
Marwan	مروان	an ancient Arab name
Marzooq	مرزوق	blessed (by God), fortunate, prosperous, successful
Mashhood	مشهود	witnessed, present, manifest, the day of judgment, the day of Arafah
Mashkoor	مشكور	the person to whom one is indebted.
Maseeh	مسيح	one who is blessed with piety from the cradle to the grave. The Messiah (Jesus), a Prophet.
Maseehuzzaman	مسيح الزمان	Masih (Messiah) of the age
Masir	مصير	destiny, goal
Masood	مسعود	prosperous, happy, dutiful, fortunate, lucky
Masoom	معصوم	innocent, sinless, infallible, protected
Masun	مصون	guarded, well-protected

Matin	متين	strong, powerful, solid, of resolute mind, durable. Al-Matin المتين the Strong: one of the names of Allah
Abdul Matin	عبد المتين	servant of the Strong i.e. Allah
Matloob	مطلوب	desired, required, sought after
Mausoof	موصوف	worthy of description, endowed with laudable qualities
Mawahib	مواهب	pl. of Mauhiba موهبة, gift, talent
Mawdood	مودود	beloved, attached
Mawhoob	موهوب	gifted, talented, endowed, favoured
Mawla	مولیٰ	helper, protector
Fazle Mawla	فضل مولیٰ	bounty of the lord (Allah)
Mazhar	مظهر	manifestation, expression, outlook
Mazhar-ud-Din	مظهر الدين	manifestation of the religion (Islam)
Mazharul Haq	مظهر الحق	manifestation of the Truth i.e. Allah.
Mazid	مزيد	increase, excess, more
Mazin	مازن	proper name
Miftah	مفتاح	key
Mimrah	ممراح	cheerful, lively, gay-tempered
Minhaj	منهاج	method, system, order, way, road
Minnat	منّة	grace, kindness, favour, gift
Minnatullah	منة الله	gratitude owed to Allah
Miqdam	مقدام	in the forefront of battle, very bold, undaunted

Mir	مير	prince, governor, leader
Miraj	معراج	place of ascent
Miran	ميران	princes; pl. of Mir مير
MirJahaan (Per)	مير جهان	king of the world
Mirsab	مِرسَب	prudent, wise, a sword of the Prophet Muhammadﷺ
Mirza (Per)	ميرزا	son of a prince. Honorific title
Misaq	ميثاق	agreement, covenent, contract, pact
Misbah	مصباح	lamp, lantern
Misbahuddin	مصباح الدين	lamp of the religion (Islam)
Mizan	ميزان	balance, scales
Mizanur Rahman	ميزان الرحمن	(Meezan al-Rahman) balance of the most merciful i.e. Allah
Muammar	معمر	antiquated, long-lived, one given long life, title of Luqman i.e. Lokman
Muawin	معاون	assistant, helper, supporter
Muayyad	مؤيد	supported, championed, approved, victorious
Muaz	معاذ	protected
Muawiyah	معاويه	a young dog or fox (first Umayyad Khalifah)
Muazzam	معظم	exalted, glorified, honoured, revered
Mubajjal	مبجل	glorified, exalted, honourable, greatly respected

Mubarak	مبارك	blessed, fortunate, lucky, auspicious, august
Mubashshir	مبشّر	bringer of good news, a Prophet
Mubin	مبين	clear, plain, distinct, manifest
Mubtasim	مبتسم	smiling
Mudabbir	مدبر	planner, designer, disposer
Muddassir	مدّثر	wrapped in, enveloped, attribute of the Prophet Muhammadﷺ
Mudrik	مدرك	perceptive, intelligent, reasonable, endowed with reason
Mufakhkhar	مفخّر	glorious, exalted
Mufazzal	مفضّل	preferred, chosen, favoured
Mufid	مفيد	beneficial, useful, advantageous, favoured, profitable
Mufiz	مفيض	giver
Mufti	مفتى	interpreter or expounder of Sharia (Islamic law)
Mughis	مغيث	helper, assistant
Mughni	مغنى	one who releases another from straitened circumstances, an epithet of Allah
Muhafiz	محافظ	preserver, custodian, guardian
Muhafiz-ud-Din محافظ الدين		preserver of the religion (Islam)
Muhajir	مهاجر	emigrant
Muhannad	مهند	sword, Indian sword

Muhammad	محمد	praised, lauded, commended, praiseworthy. Muhammad ibn Abdullah (570-632): Messenger of Allah who preached the faith of Islam
Muhaimin	مهيمن	ruler, overlord, one who provides sanctuary from any hazard or danger. Al-Muhaimin المهيمن the All-preserver: one of the names of Allah
Abdul Muhaimin عبد المهيمن		servant of the All-preserver
Muhazzab	مهذّب	polite, courteous, well-mannered
Muhib	محبّ	loving, affectionate, friend
Muhibuddin	محب الدين	friend of the religion (Islam)
Mhibbullah	محب الله	friend of Allah
Muhit	محيط	encompassing, ocean
Muhsin	محسن	benevolent, benefactor, charitable, humanitarian
Muhtadi	المهتدى	rightly guided, following the right path, on the right way
Muhtashim	محتشم	decent, modest, chaste, shy
Muhyi	محيى	one who gives life, reviver
Muhiyuddin	محيى الدين	reviver of the religion (Islam)
Muid	معيد	reviser, restore
Abdul Muid	عبد المعيد	servant of the Restorer i.e. Allah
Muin	معين	helper, patron, supporter, aide.

Muinuddin	معين الدين	helper of the religion (Islam)
Muinul Islam	معين الاسلام	supporter of Islam
Muinuddawlah	معين الدولة	defender of the state
Muizz	معزّ	one who honours, strengthens
Muizzuddin	معزّ الدين	one who strengthens the religion (Islam)
Muizzuddawlah	معز الدولة	he who renders the state mighty
Mujahid	مجاهد	one who struggles, strives, or fights for the cause of Islam, soldier of jihad
Mujammil	مجمل	adorner, beautifier
Mujib	مجيب	replier, answerer. Allah's epithet
Abdul Mujib	عبد المجيب	servant of the Answerer i.e. Allah
Mujir	مجير	protector, defender, helper, supporter
Mujtaba	مجتبى	chosen, selected, elected. Title of the Prophet Muhammadﷺ
Mujtahid	مجتهد	diligent, industrious, hardworking
Mukafih	مكافح	freedom fighter
Mukammil	مكمل	perfecting, completing
Mukarram	مكرّم	honoured, revered, honourable, noble
Mukhallad	مخلّد	immortal
Mukhlis	مخلص	sincere, honest, true, faithful
Mukhtar	مختار	selected, chosen, preferred, favourite, the most exquisite.

Mukhtarul Haq	مختار الحق	chosen by the Truth i.e. Allah.
Mukrram	مكرم	one who is honoured
Muktafi	مكتفى	satisfied, contended
Mulham	ملهم	inspired
Mulk	ملك	kingdom, sovereignty, supreme power or authority
Saifulmulk	سيف الملك	sword of the kingdom
Mulla	ملاّ	A Persian construction probably from the Arabic Mawla ('master', 'leader', 'lord')
Mumin	مؤمن	believer (in Islam), pious, one who advocates peace and harmony. Allah's attribute.
Abdul Mu'min	عبد المؤمن	servant of the All-faithful i.e. Allah
Mumtaz	ممتاز	distinguished, superior, outstanding
Munadil	مناضل	fighter, defender
Munaim	مناعم	"benevolent kind" Al-Muna'im المناعم, the Benevolent: one of the names of the Allah
Munasir	مناصر	helper, protector, friend
Munawwar	منور	illuminated, brilliant
Mani	منيع	strong, secure, well-fortified, unconquerable
Munib	منيب	one who turns to Allah seeking His pardon
Munif	منيف	eminent, exalted, superior, high, lofty
Munim	منعم	benefactor, donor, grantor

Abdul-Munim	عبد المنعم	servant of the benefactor i.e. Allah
Munir	منير	splendid, shining, something that reflects light, bright, brilliant, radiant, luminous.
Muniruzzaman	منير الزمان	brilliant of the age
Munis	مونس	sociable, friendly, kind, gentle
Munjid	منجد	helper, supporter, rescuer
Munna	مِنَّة	strength, power, vigour
Munqiz	منقذ	saviour, rescuer, deliverer
Munsif	منصف	just, fair, righteous
Muntasir	منتصر	victorious, triumphant
Muntazar	منتظر	expected, prospective, anticipated, awaited
Munzir	منذر	warner, cautioner, forerunner. Messenger sent by Allah to warn mankind
Muqarrab	مقرب	intimate companion, friend, one who is brought near the throne of Allah, one who is nearest to Allah
Muqeet	مقيت	provider. Al-Muqeetالمقيت, the Nourisher: one of the names of Allah
Muqla	مقلة	eye, eyeball, the middle of anything. Ibn Muqlah (886-940); Abbasid vizier and "founder of Arabic calligraphy"
Muqsit	مقسط	just, impartial, Allah's attribute
Muqtadi	مقتدى	follower, one who follows an imam during ritual prayer

Muqtadir	مقتدر	able, powerful, mighty, Allah's epithet. Al-Muqtadirالمقتدر, the omnipotent: one of the names of Allah
Abdul Muqtadir عبد المقتدر		('abd al-muqtadir): servant of the Omnipotent i.e. Allah
Muqtafi	مقتفى	one who follows (another). Al-Muqtafi (1136-60): Abbasid Khalifa
Muqtasid	مقتصد	frugal, thrifty, economical
Murad	مراد	will, intention, desire, intended
Murshid	مرشد	leader, guide, adviser, counsellor
Murtaza	مرتضى	chosen, approved, agreeable, acceptable, an epithet of the Prophet Muhammad ﷺ
Musa	موسى	a Prophet, the biblical Moses
Musad	مسعد	fortunate, lucky, unfettered camel
Musaddiq	مصدق	one who confirms. One who accepts another's word as truth
Musaid	مساعد	helper, assistant, supporter
Musawwir	مصور	shaper, fashioner
Abdul Musawwirعبد المصور		(abd Al-Musawwir): servant of the Fashioner i.e. Allah
Musharraf	مشرَّف	honoured, exalted
Musharrif	مشرِّف	one who exalts
Mushfiq	مشفق	kind, tender, fearful
Mushir	مشير	counsellor, advisor

Mushir-ul-Haq	مشير الحق	counsellor of the Truth i.e. Allah
Mushtaq	مشتاق	longing, desiring, eager
Musir	موسر	properous, affluent, rich
Muslih	مصلح	peacemaker, conciliator, reformer, one who sets things right
Muslihuddin	مصلح الدين	reformer of the religion (Islam)
Muslim	مسلم	follower of the religion of Islam.
Mustafa	مصطفیٰ	chosen, selected, preferred
Mustafavi	مصطفوی	attributed to the family of Mustafa, i.e. Muhammadﷺ
Mustafiz	مستفيض	profitting, one who is desirous of gaining
Mustahfiz	مستحفظ	guardian, protector, custodian
Mustain	مستعين	one who asks the help or aid or assistance
Mustakfi	مستكفى	one who desires another to do something effectively
Mustali	مستعلى	high, elevated, superior
Mustamsik	مستمسك	composed, calm of mind, one who restrains himself
Mustanjid	مستنجد	one who implores for help
Mustansir	مستنصر	one who asks for help
Mustaqim	مستقيم	straight, upright
Mustarshid	مسترشد	one who seeks direction
Mustasim	مستعصم	he who holds fast

Mustazhir	مستظهر	memoriser, one who knows by heart
Mustazi	مستضئ	one who seeks light or advice or guidance
Mutali	متعالى	exalted, supreme
Abdul Mutali	عبد المتعالى	servant of the most High i.e. Allah
Mutad	معتد	prepared, ready
Mutahhar	مطهّر	pure, clean, purified, very beautiful
Mutamad	معتمد	trustworthy, reliable, dependable
Mutamid	معتمد	one who relies (upon Allah)
Mutamin	مؤتمن	one who entrusts his affairs to the management of another
Mutammim	متمّم	perfecting, completing
Mutaqid	معتقد	confident, believer, faithful friend
Mutasim	معتصم	abstaining from sin (by the grace of Allah), preserved, defended
Mutawakkil	متوكل	one who puts his trust (in Allah)
Mutawassit	متوسّط	mediator, umpire
Mutazid	معتضد	one who takes assistance (of Allah), petitioner of justice
Mutazz	معتزّ	mighty, proud, powerful
Muta	مطاع	obeyed
Muti	معطى	giver, granter, donor, المعطى Al-Mu'ti, the Granter: one of the names of Allah
Abdul Muti	عبد المعطى	servant of the Donor i.e. Allah

Muti'	مطيع	obedient, pious, devoted, faithful, submissive
Mutiul Islam	مطيع الاسلام	obedient (follower) of Islam
Mutiur Rahman	مطيع الرحمن	(muti' al-Rahman) obedient (servant) of the most gracious i.e. Allah
Mutlaq	مطلق	free, unlimited, unrestricted
Muttalib	مطّلب	seeker. Abdul Muttalib: grandfather of the Prophet Muhammad صلى الله عليه وسلم
Muttaqi	المتقى	(al-Muttaqi) God-fearing, pious, religious, devout
Muwaffaq	موفّق	successful, prosperous, lucky, fortunate
Muzaffar	مظفّر	victorious, triumphant, conqueror
Muzaffaruddin	مظفر الدين	victorious of the religion (Islam)
Muzahir	مظاهر	protector, defender, supporter
Muzahiruddin	مظاهر الدين	defender of the religion (Islam)
Muzakkir	مذكّر	reminder, warner
Muzammil	مزّمّل	one who is enwrapped in garments. al-Muzzammil المزّمّل: title of the 73rd Sura of the Qur'an. In this sura, Allah addresses the Prophet Muhammad صلى الله عليه وسلم

N

Nabih	نابه	noble, famous, eminent, distinguished, brilliant

Naif	نائف	exalted, lofty, eminent, superior
Nail	نائل	winner, gainer
Naji	ناجى	saved, liberated, safe
Najillah	ناجى الله	saved by Allah. An epithet of Prophet Nuh
Najih	ناجح	successful, prosperous
Nashit	ناشط	energetic, dynamic, lively, fresh, vigorous
Nassi	ناصع	clear, pure, white
Nasir	ناصر	helper, protector, defender
Abdun Nasir	عبد الناصر	servant of the Helper i.e. Allah
Nasiruddin	ناصر الدين	defender of the faith (Islam)
Nazir	ناضر	bright, radiant, blooming
Nabi	نبيّ	Prophet sent by Allah for the guidance of mankind
Nabiullah	نبى الله	an epithet of the Prophet Nuh
Nabi Bakhsh	نبى بخش	gift of the Prophet
Nabih	نبيه	famous, noble, outstanding, eminent, distiguished, brilliant
Nabil	نبيل	noble, highborn, honourable, intelligent, dexterous, one skilled in archery
Nadim	نديم	intimate friend, boon companion, courtier
Nadir	نادر	extraordinary, rare, dear, exceptional
Nafi	نافع	beneficial, advantageous, profitable

Nafis	نفيس	refined, pure, choice, exquisite, precious, invaluable, costly
Naib	نائب	deputy
Naim	نعيم	happiness, comfort, ease, tranquil, felicity, peaceful, bliss, pleasure, bounty, anything given as gift
Aynun Naim	عين النعيم	fountain of blessing
Naimullah	نعيم	grace of Allah, bliss of Allah
Najah	نجاح	success
Najat	نجات	rescue, salvation, deliverance
Naji	نجىّ	intimate friend, bosom freind
Najiullah	نجى الله	intimate friend of Allah
Najib	نجيب	excellent, noble, distinguished, praiseworthy, generous, aristocratic
Najibullah	نجيب الله	distinguished (servant) of Allah
Najib-ud-Din	نجيب الدين	distinguished (person) of religion (Islam)
Najih	نجيح	sound, good (opinion)
Najm	نجم	star, planet
Najmuddawlah	نجم الدوله	star of the state
Najmuddin	نجم الدين	star of the religion (Islam)
Nameer	نمير	pure, clear, healthy, good
Namir	نمر	leopard, tiger, panther
Naqi	نقى	pure, clean

Naqib	نقيب	president, head, chief
Nashit	نشيط	energetic, dynamic, lively, fresh, vigorous
Nashwan	نشوان	elated, exalted, exuberant
Nasib	نسيب	noble, highborn
Nasif	ناصف	just
Nasih	ناصح	adviser, counsellor
Nasihuddin	ناصح الدين	counsellor of the religion (Islam)
Nasim	نسيم	gentle wind, fresh air, fragrant air, zephyr, a cool breeze
Nasimuddin	نسيم الدين	breeze of the religion (Islam)
Nasim-ul-Haq	نسيم الحق	breeze of the Truth i.e. Allah
Nasir	نصير	helper, protector, patron
Nasiruddin	نصير الدين	defender of the religion (Islam)
Nasr	نصر	help, aid, support
Nasrullah	نصر الله	help of Allah
Nasruddin	نصر الدين	victory of the religion (Islam)
Nasri	نصرى	winner of victory after victory
Natiq	ناطق	endowed with speech, eloquent, rational (being), spokesperson
Nawed (Per)	نويد	happy tidings, good news
Nawaz (Per)	نواز	one who caresses, soothes
Shah Nawaz (Per)	شاه نواز	friend of king

Nawfal	نوفل	generous, old Arabic name for the sea
Naif	نيف	excess, surplus
Nazir	نذير	warner, Prophet sent by Allah to warn mankind, a courtier
Nazif	نظيف	pure, clean, innocent, neat and clean, chaste
Nazih	نزيه	pure, virtuous, just, honest
Nazim	ناظم	organiser, governor, arranger, adjuster, administrator, director, a composer of verses
Nazimuddin	ناظم الدين	organiser of the religion (Islam)
Nazir	نظير	precedent, alike, equal to
Nazmi	نظمى	arranger, organiser
Nazr	نذر	a vow, promise made to God; a gift, charity, votive offering
Nimat	نعمت	blessing, boon, favour, grace, bounty, comforts of life
Nimatullah	نعمت الله	blessing of Allah
Nisar	نثار	to strew, to sacrifice
Nizal	نضال	striving, contest, competition, battle
Nizam	نظام	order, arrangement, discipline, ruler, system
Nizamuddin	نظام الدين	discipline of the religion (Islam)
Nizam-ul-Mulk	نظام الملك	the organisation of the kingdom
Nizami	نظامى	of or relating to Nizam

Nuaym	نُعَيم	diminutive of Naaimناعم, gentle, delicate
Nuh	نوح	Noah, name of Prophet of Allah
Numan	نعمان	Blood; name of the king of Hirah in Arabia, especially of the last, Numan bin Munzir, also name of a *sahabi (AS)*
Noor	نور	light, illumination. Allah's epithet
Abdun Noor	عبد النور	servant of the Light
Noorullah	نور الله	light of Allah
Noor Muhammad	نور محمد	light of the Prophet Muhammad ﷺ
Nooruddin	نور الدين	light of the religion (Islam)
Noorul Haq	نور الحق	light of the Truth i.e. Allah
Nooruzzaman	نور الزمان	light of the era
Noori	نوريّ	light, luminous
Nusrat	نصرت	help, aid, assistance, support
Nusratuddin	نصرت الدين	help of the religion (Islam)
Nuzayh	نزيه	pure, chaste

O

Obaidullah	عبيد الله	See Ubaidullah
Osman	عثمان	See Usman (*Uthmaan*)
Omar	عمر	See Umar

P

Pasha (Tur)	باشا	lord, honorific title
Parvez (Per)	پرویز	victorious, fortunate, happy
Pir (Per)	پیر	saint, spritual guide, wise

Q

Qadir	قادر	able, capable, powerful, mighty. One of the names of Allah
Abdul Qadir	عبد القادر	servant of the Powerful i.e. Allah
Qabil	قابیل	son of Adam
Qadir	قدیر	able, powerful, mighty, one of the names of Allah
Abdul Qadir	عبد القدیر	servant of the Powerful i.e. Allah
Qahir	قاهر	conqueror, subduer
Abdul Qahir	عبدالقاهر	servant of the Subduer i.e. Allah
Qaid	قائد	leader, commander
Qaim	قائم	upright, independent, one who performs
Qais	قیس	measure, measurement, firm, example
Qaiser	قیصر	caesar
Qamar	قمر	the moon. Al-Qamar القمر: title of 54th sura of the Qur'an

Qamaruddin	قمر الدين	moon of the religion (Islam)
Qasid	قاصد	messenger, courier
Qasidul Haq	قاصد الحق	courier of the Truth i.e. Allah
Qasim	قاسم	distributor, divider
Abul Qasim	ابو القاسم	father of Qasim, an attributive name of the Prophet Muhammad ﷺ
Qatadah	قتادة	Astragalus, a hardwood tree
Qawi	قوىّ	strong, powerful, firm, mighty. One of the names of Allah
Abdul Qawi	عبد القوى	servant of the Mighty i.e. Allah
Qayyum	قيوم	eternal, everlasting. An epithet applied to Allah
Abdul Qayyuam	عبد القيوم	servant of the Eternal i.e. Allah
Qazi	القاضى	judge, justice
Qudwa	قدوة	model, example
Qismat	قسمت	fate, destiny
Qiwam	قوام	support, prop
Qiwamuddin	قوام الدين	support of the religion (Islam)
Quddoos	قدّوس	holy, most, pure, free from any defects. Al-Quddus القدوس, the All-holy: one of the names of Allah
Abdul Quddus	عبد القدوس	servant of the All-holy
Qudrat	قدرت	power, might, strength

Qudratullah	قدرت الله	power of Allah
Quds	قدس	holiness, sanctity
Qudsi	قدسی	holy, sacred
Qudus	قدُس	holiness, sanctity
Ruhul Qudus	روح القدُس	an epithet of Jibreel i.e. Gabriel
Quraishi	قریشی	attributed to Quraish, the tribe of the Prophet Muhammad
Qurban	قربان	sacrifice, sacrifice on the occasion of Eid-al-adha
Qutaiba	قتیبة	irritable, impatient
Qutb	قطب	leader, chief, pivot, axis, pole
Qutbuddin	قطب الدین	leader of the religion (Islam)

R

Rai	راعی	guardian, custodian, patron, protector, sponsor
Raid	رائد	pioneer, explorer, leader, model
Raiq	رائق	pure, ciear, tranquil, serene
Raji	راجی	hopeful, hoping, full of hope
Razi	راضی	satisfied, contended, well-pleased
Rabah	رباح	gain, profit
Rab	ربّ	lord, master. One of the names of Allah

Abdur Rab	عبد الرب	servant of the Lord, i.e. Allah
Rabbani	ربانى	divine, from Allah
Fazle Rab	فضل رب	bounty of Lord
Rabi	ربيع	spring, springtime
Rabia	ربيعة	fem. of Rabi
Rabih	رابح	winner, gainer
Rafi'	رفيع	high ranking, noble, eminent, exalted, sublime
Al-Rafi'	الرفيع	one of the names of Allah
Abdul Rafi	عبدالرفيع	servant of the Exalted i.e. Allah
Rafi-ud-Din	رفيع الدين	noble (person) of the religion (Isalm)
Rafid	رافد	tributary stream, affluent, helper, supporter, aide
Rafif	رفيف	glittering, shining, gleaming.
Rafiq	رفيق	associate, intimate friend, companion.
Rafiqul Islam	رفيق الاسلام	friend of Islam
Raghib	راغب	willing, desirous, wishful, inclined towards...anything
Ragheed	رغيد	comfort, opulence, affluence
Rahim	رحيم	merciful, compassionate, kind. Al-Rahim الرحيم, the most Merciful: one of the names of Allah
Abdur Rahim	عبد الرحيم	servant of the most Merciful i.e. Allah

Rahman	رحمٰن	Al-Rahman الرحمٰن, the most Gracious; one of the names of Allah
Abdur Rahman	عبد الرحمٰن	servant of the most Gracious i.e. Allah
Rahmat	رحمت	sympathy, mercy, compassion, kindness
Rahmatullah	رحمت الله	mercy of Allah
Rais	رئيس	leader, chief, president, superior, nobleman
Raisuddin	رئيس الدين	leader of the religion (Islam)
Raja	رجاء	hope, wish
Raja al-Karim	رجاء الكريم	hope of the Kind
Rajab	رجب	the seventh month of the Islamic calendar.
Ramiz	رامز	one who indicates by signs
Ramiz-ud-Din	رامز الدين	one who indicates by signs to the religion (Islam)
Raqib	رقيب	observer, guard. الرقيب, the Watcher: one of the names of Allah
Abdur Raqib	عبد الرقيب	servant of the Observer, i.e. Allah
Rashad	رشاد	to lead a righteous life, right guidance, integrity of conduct
Rashid	راشد	right-minded, rightly-guided, pious
Rashiduddin	راشد الدين	rightly-guided (person) of the religion (Islam)
Rashid	رشيد	wise, prudent, judicious, rightly guided. Al-Rasheed الرشيد, the Right-minded: one of the names of Allah

Abdur Rashid	عبد الرشيد	servant of the Right-minded i.e. Allah
Rashid-ud-din	رشيد الدين	wise (person) of the faith (Islam)
Rashiq	رشيق	graceful, elegant
Rasikh	راسخ	well-established, well-founded, stable, steady
Rasim	راسم	planner, designer
Rasin	رصين	calm, composed
Rasul	رسول	messenger, messenger of Allah
Ratib	راتب	arranger
Rauf	رؤوف	merciful, kind, compassionate. الرؤوف, the most Kind: one of the names of Allah
Abdur Rauf	عبد الرؤوف	servant of the most Kind i.e. Allah
Rayhan	ريحان	ease, fragrant herb, sweet basil, comfort.
Razi	رضى	satisfied, contended, pleased
Razin	رزين	calm, composed, self-possessed
Razzaq	رزّاق	provider. Al-Razzaaqالرزاق, the All-provider: one of the names of Allah
Abdur Razzaq	عبد الرزاق	servant of the All-provider i.e. Allah
Reza	رضا	contentment, satisfaction, pleasure, approval, consent.
Rezaul Karim	رضاء الكريم	satisfaction of the most Generous (Allah)
Rif'at	رفعت	high rank, high standing, dignity, exaltation, eminence

Rifaat	رفاعة	name of twenty three companions of Muhammad ﷺ
Riyaz	رياض	pl. of Rawza روضة garden
Riyazul Islam	رياض الاسلام	gardens of Islam
Rizq/Rizk	رزق	livelihood, subsistence, blessing of Allah
Rizk Allah	رزق الله	livelihood from Allah
Rizwaan	رضوان	satisfaction contentment, happiness, pleasure, name of the Keeper of the gates of *Jannah* (Paradise)
Rooh/Ruh	روح	spirit, soul
Roohullah	روح الله	(ruh allah): spirit of Allah. An epithet of Prophet 'Isa
Roohul Amin	روح الامين	spirit of the faithful, spirit of the reliable; an epithet of Jibreel
Ruhul Haq	روح الحق	spirit of the truth. An epithet of the Prophet Muhammad ﷺ
Ruhul Qudus	روح القدس	sprit of the holy. Epithet of Jibreel i.e. Gabriel
Rukn	ركن	pillar, prop, support
Ruknud din	ركن الدين	pillar of the religion (Islam)
Rushd	رشد	right guidance
Rustam	رستم	the most renowned hero among the Persians, hero of the persian epic 'Shahnama'
Ruwwad	رواد	pioneers, explorers, guides, leaders, models; pl. of Raid رائد

S

Sabih	صابح	coming or arrival in the morning
Sabir	صابر	patient, tolerant
Sadaat	سادات	princes, lords, chiefs, title of the Prophet Muhammad's ﷺ direct descendents
Anwarus Sadat	أنور السادات	most brilliant of the chiefs
Ashrafus Sadat	أشرف السادات	most noble of the Sayyids
Iftikharus Sadat	افتخار السادات	pride of the chiefs
Sadiq	صادق	true, truthful, honest, sincere, devoted, faithful, veracious
Safi	صافى	pure, clear, crystal
Sahir	ساهر	wakeful
Said	صاعد	rising, ascending
Saim	صائم	fasting
Salim	سالم	safe, secure, perfect, complete
Sami	سامى	eminent, exalted, high-minded, sublime
Samir	ثامر	fruit-bearing, fruitful, productive
Sabah	صباح	morning
Sabat	ثبات	firmness, stability, certainty, endurance, boldness, truth
Sabih	صبيح	beautiful, handsome, one with a fair complexion

Sabeer	صبير	patient, tolerant
Sabiq	سابق	first, winner
Sabit	ثابت	strong, well-established, certain, sure
Sabuh	صبوح	shining, brilliant
Saboor	صبور	patient, tolerant, forebearing
Abdussaboor	عبد الصبور	(Abd-al-Saboor) servant of the Patient i.e. Allah
Saadat	سعادت	prosperity, happiness, good fortune, auspiciousness
Saad	سعد	good luck, good fortune, success, happiness, prosperity, lucky
Saeed	سعيد	fortunate, auspicious, venerable, dignified, happy, lucky
Abu Saeed	ابو سعيد	father of dignified, name of a *sahabi* (RA)
Saeeduz Zaman	سعيد الزمان	luckiest of the age
Saaduddin	سعد الدين	success of the religion (Islam)
Saadullah	سعدالله	joy of Allah
Saadi	سعدى	happy, lucky, blissful fortunate, name of a great Persian poet
Sadid	سديد	correct, right, sound, appropriate, unerring, hitting the target
Sadiq	صديق	friend, companion
Sadr	صدر	chest, breast, forefront, start, dawn, bosom, the highest part, prime

Sadruddin	صدر الدين	(person at) forefront of the faith (Islam)
Saduh	صدوح	singer, singing
Sadooq	صدوق	honest, truthful, sincere, trustworthy
Safdar	صفدر	brave, a violent warrior
Saffah	سفاح	killer, bloodshedder
Safi	صفى	pure, just, righteous, pious
Safiullah	صفى الله	the pure (one) of Allah
Safiuddin	صفىّ الدين	the pure (one) of the faith (Islam)
Safir	سفير	ambassador, mediator, intercessor
Safwan	صفوان	pure, clear, smooth stone, cloudless day
Saghir	صغير	small, young, slender, tender
Saghir Ali	صغير على	little Ali
Sahab	سحاب	clouds
Sahl	سهل	soft, soil, smooth, simple, facile, easy, even
Sajid	ساجد	prostrate in worship, bowing in adoration to Allah
Sajidur Rahman	ساجد الرحمٰن	one who prostrates to the Merciful (Allah)
Sajjad	سجاد	one who constantly prostrates, worshipper of Allah, worshipper engaged in sujud (prostration) before Allah
Sakha	سخاء	generosity, liberality
Sakhawat	سخاوت	generosity, liberality

Salabat	صلابت	strong, majesty, dignity, awe
Salah	صلاح	piety, righteousness, honesty, goodness, peace, concord, treaty, rectitude
Salah-ud-Din	صلاح الدين	rectitude of the faith (Islam)
Salam	سلام	peace, safety, security. Al-Salam السلام, the All-peaceable: one of the names of Allah
Abdussalam	عبد السلام	servant of the All-peaceable
Salama	سلمة	peace; fem. of Salam سلم
Salamat	سلامت	safety, security, soundness, integrity
Salamatullah	سلامت الله	security of Allah
Salik	سالك	traveller, wayfarer
Salih	صالح	pious, righteous, upright, just, virtuous, devoted, chaste
Salil	سليل	drawn (sword), scion, son
Salim	سالم	safe, sound, perfect, complete
Salim	سليم	sound, affable, healthy, guarded, perfect, complete, safe, secure
Salimullah	سليم الله	soundest (servant) of Allah
Salimuz Zaman	سليم الزمان	soundest (person) of the time
Salit	سليط	strong, solid, firm, sharp
Salman	سلمان	safe, mild, affable, perfect, name of a *sahabi* i.e. companion of the Prophet Muhammadﷺ

Samad	صمد	eternal, high, Al-Samad الصمد, the Everlasting: one of the names of Allah
Abdus Samad	عبد الصمد	servant of the Eternal
Samah	سماح	generosity, bounty, good-heartedness
Sami'	سميع	hearing, listening. Al-Sami' السميع, the All-Hearing: one of the names of Allah
Abdussami	عبد السميع	servant of the All-hearing i.e. Allah
Samih	سميح	magnanimous, generous, king, forgiving, good-hearted
Samim	صميم	sincere, genuine, pure, true, essence, heart
Samin	ثمين	valuable, precious, priceless
Samir	سمير	companion (in nightly conversation), entertainer (with stories, music etc.)
Saamir	سامر	entertainer
Sana	ثناء	praise, commendation, eulogy
Sanaullah	ثناء الله	praise of Allah
Sanad	سند	support, prop
Sanie	سنىّ	brilliant, majestic, exalted, eminent, splendid
Saqib	ثاقب	penetrating, piercing, sharp-witted, sagacious, astute, acute
Saqif	ثقيف	proficient, skilful
Sardar (Per)	سردار	chief, noble man, officer of rank
Sarkar (Per)	سركار	chief, overseer

Sarwar	سرور	leader, chief, master
Sattar	ستار	veiler (of sin). Al-Sattar الستار, the veiler of sin: one of the names of Allah
Saulat	صولت	pomp, dignity, majesty
Saud	سعود	fortunate, pious, auspicious, prosperous
Abdus Sattar	عبدالستار	servant of the Veiler of sin i.e. Allah
Saif	سيف	sword
Saifullah	سيف الله	sword of Allah. Title of honour awarded to Khalid ibn Walid by the Prophet Muhammadﷺ
Saifuddin	سيف الدين	sword of the religion (Islam)
Saiful Islam	سيف الاسلام	sword of Islam
Sayyid	سيِّد	lord, master, chief
Shafi	شافى	healing, one who cures, salutary, satisfactory
Shafi	شافع	intercessor, mediator
Shahid	شاهد	witness, angel
Shaban	شعبان	Eighth lunar month. It is a month of religious significance for Muslims
Shabbar	شبر	son of the Prophet Harun, by which name Muhammadﷺ is said to have called his grandson Hasan
Shabbir	شبير	son of Prophet Harun, by which name Muhammadﷺ is said to have called his grandson Husain

Shad	شاد	happy
Shadi	شادی	singer
Shafaat	شفاعت	intercession, mediation, recommendation
Shafqat	شفقت	compassion, pity, kindness, tenderness
Shafi	شفیع	intercessor, mediator
Shafiq	شفیق	affectionate, compassionate, tender, kind-hearted friend, warm-hearted
Shah (Per)	شاہ	king, emperor. Title assumed by fakirs i.e. mystics
Shah Alam	شاہ عالم	king of the world
Shahbaz	شاہ باز	royal falcon, royal, generous, noble
Shah Jahan	شاہ جہان	king of the world
Shah Nawaaz	شاہ نواز	friend of king
Shahzada	شاہ زادہ	prince
Shahadat	شہادت	testimony, evidence, fundamental belief in Islam
Shahan	شاہان	kings; pl. of Shah شاہ, king
Shahan Shah	شاہان شاہ	king of kings
Shaheed	شہید	present, witness, martyr in the cause of Islam and as such held in very high esteem and honour
Shahin (Per)	شاہین	royal, white falcon; the needle of the beam of scales
Shahiq	شاہق	high, towering, lofty, tall

Shahir	شاهر	famous, eminent, renowned
Shahryar	شهریار	friend of the city
Shaikh	شيخ	chief, an experienced man, an old man
Shaikhul Islam	شيخ الاسلام	leader of Islam
Shajaat	شجاعت	courage, bravery, valour
Shaji	شجيع	courageous, bold, brave, fearless
Shakil	شكيل	well formed, handsome, comely, well-shaped
Shakir	شاكر	thankful, grateful, contented
Shakur	شكور	thankful, most grateful, one who gives due appreciation. Al-Shakur الشكور, the All-thankful; one of the names of Allah
Abdus Shakoor	عبد الشكور	servant of the All-thankful i.e. Allah
Shams	شمس	the sun
Shamsuddin	شمس الدين	son of the religion (Islam)
Shamsheer (Per)	شمشير	sword
Shamim	شميم	fragrant, scent, a sweet-smelling breeze
Sharaf	شرف	nobility, high rank, eminence, honour distinction, honour, glory, dignity
Sharafuddin	شرف الدين	honour of the religion (Islam)
Sharafat	شرافت	honour, nobleness
Shariat	شريعت	divine law, Islamic law
Shariatullah	شريعت الله	divine law of Allah

Sharif	شريف	noble, honourable, highborn, eminent
Sharifuddin	شريف الدين	noble (person) of the religion (Islam)
Shawkat	شوكت	power, might, valour, dignity, magnificence, grandeur, pomp, power
Shaikh	شيخ	title of a political or spiritual leader of a muslim community; chief, head, old man
Sher (Per)	شير	lion, An epithet of Khalifa Ali
Shibl	شبل	lion cub
Shihab	شهاب	flame, meteor, shooting star, star
Shihabuddin	شهاب الدين	meteor of the religion (Islam)
Shiqdar (Per)	شقدار	land tax collector during the Muslim rule in India, now a family title
Shua	شعاع	ray of the sun, sunshine, light, lustre, splendour
Shuauddin	شعاع الدين	rays of the religion (Islam)
Shuaib	شعيب	a Prophet (see surat al-A'raaf 7:88)
Shubool	شبول	lion cubs; pl. of Shibl شبل
Shuhrat/Shuhrah	شهرت	fame, renown
Shuja	شجاع	courageous, bold, brave
Shujauddin	شجاع الدين	brave (person) of the religion, (Islam)
Shukr	شكر	thanks, gratitude, gratefulness
Siddiq	صديق	righteous, very truthful, honest, sincere
Al-Siddiq	الصديق	the truthful, title of Abu Bakr the first righteous Caliph

Siddiqullah	صديق الله	the truthful (one) to Allah. An epithet of Prophet Yusuf.
Siddiqi	صديقيّ	attributed to the first Khalifa Abu Bakr Al-Siddiq (d. 634) through ancestry
Siham	سهام	arrows; pl. of Sahm سهم
Sikandar (Per)	سكندر	Alexander
Silah	سِلاح	arms, armour, weapons
Silahuddin	سلاح الدين	armour of the religion (Islam)
Silm	سلم	peace
Sinan	سنان	spear. Umm Sinan: a sahaabia i.e. a woman who lived in Prophet Muhammad's time
Sinanuddin	سنان الدين	spear of the religion (Islam)
Siraj	سراج	lamp, light, the sun, candle
Sirajud Dawlah	سراج الدوله	lamp of the state
Sirajuddin	سراج الدين	lamp of the religion (Islam)
Somood	ثمود	Steadfastness, firmness, endurance
Subah	صباح	beautiful, graceful
Subbooh	سبّوح	extremely pure, Allah's attribute.
Subahuddin	صباح الدين	beautiful (person) of the religion (Islam)
Subhan	سبحان	praise, glory. Al-Subhaan السبحان, the Glory: one of the names of Allah.
Abdussubhan	عبد السبحان	servant of the Glory i.e. Allah

Subhi	صبحى	pertaining to morning
Sufi	صوفىّ	a mystic, someone believing in Sufi mysticism
Sufian	سفيان	ship builder. Abu Sufian: name of a companion of the Prophet Muhammad ﷺ
Suhaib	صهيب	of reddish hair or complexion
Suhail	سهيل	Canopus, The second brightest star in the sky
Suhrab (Per)	سهراب	son of the Iranian epic hero Rustam
Sulaiman	سليمان	a Prophet, the biblical Solomon, son of Prophet Dawood
Sultan	سلطان	king, emperor, ruler, authority, power. Title of a Muslim king

T

Taai	طائع	obedient, willing
Tabassum	تبسّم	smile
Tafazzul	تفضّل	courteousness, favour kindness, beneficence
Tafazzul Husain	تفضّل حسين	favour of Husain
Taha	طه	mystic letters at the beginning of Surat Ta Ha (20:1), from which the sura derives its title
Tahir	طاهر	virtuous, pure, pious, modest, clean, chest.

Al-Tahir	الطاهر	nickname of Abdullah, son of Muhammadﷺ who died in infancy
Tahmid	تحميد	praising Allah, saying al-hamdu lillaah الحمد لله
Tahsin	تحسين	adornment, ornament, decoration, embellishment, betterment
Taib	تائب	repentant, penitent
Taif	طيف	vision, spectre
Taifur Rahman	طيف الرحمٰن	vision of the Merciful i.e. Allah
Taisir	تيسير	making easy, facilitating, simplification
Taj	تاج	crown
Tajuddin	تاج الدين	crown of the religion (Islam)
Tajul Islam	تاج الاسلام	crown of Islam
Tajammul Husain	تجمل حسين	adornment of Husain
Talal	طلال	being pleasant, nice, admirable, agreeable, joy, a beautiful...form or appearance
Talat	طلعت	appearance, countenance
Talha	طلحة	name of a Sahabi (RA) i.e. a companion of the Prophet Muhammadﷺ
Talib	طالب	student, seeker, pursuer
Talim	تعليم	education, instruction
Tamim	تعميم	generalisation
Tamir	تامر	rich or abounding in dates, date seller

Tamiz	تمييز	distinction, distinguishing, judgment, discrimination
Tamiz-ud-Din	تميز الدين	distinction of the religion (Islam)
Tamjid	تمجيد	praise, glorification, extolment
Tanvir	تنوير	illumination, blossoming
Tanzil	تنزيل	revelation, sending down
Tanzilur Rahman	تنزيل الرحمن	revelation of the Merciful (Allah)
Taqi	تقىّ	godfearing, devout, pious
Taqiuddin	تقىّ الدين	Godfearing (person) of the religion (Islam)
Tarfa	طرفه	kind of tree
Tarib	طرب	lively, gleeful, merry
Tarif	طريف	rare, uncommon, strange, curious
Tariq	طارق	nocturnal visitor
Tarub	طروب	lively, gleeful, merry
Tasadduq	تصدّق	benificence, benevolence
Tasadduq Husain	تصدق حسين	benevolence of Husain
Taslim	تسليم	greeting, salutation
Tawfiq	توفيق	prosperity, good luck, good-fortune, success (granted by Allah)
Tawhid	توحيد	belief in the unity of Allah
Tawqir	توقير	honour, great respect, high regard

Tawwab	تواب	merciful, forgiving. Al-Tawwaabالتواب, the All-compassionate: one of the names of Allah
Abdut Tawwab	عبد التواب	servant of the most Forgiving (i.e. Allah)
Taimullah	تيم الله	servant of Allah
Tayyib	طيّب	good, good-natured, generous, sweet, pure, chaste, good-tempered
Al-Tayyib	الطيّب	nickname of Abdullah, son of Muhammadﷺ who died in infancy
Tazim	تعظيم	glorification, exaltation, honour
Tazimuddin	تعظيم الدين	glorification of the religion (Islam)
Tirmizi	الترمذى	Abu Isa Muhammad al-Tirmidhi (824-92): compiler of one collection of Prophet Muhammadﷺ
Tufail	طفيل	intercession, mediation, diminutive of Tifl طفل, baby
Turab	تراب	soil, dust
Abu Turab	أبو تراب	An attributive of Caliph Ali, the fourth of the 'rightly guided' Caliphs. The Prophet Muhammadﷺ gave him this epithet

U

Ubadah	عبادة	name of a prominent *Sahabi* i.e. companion of the Prophet Muhammadﷺ
Ubaid	عبيد	diminutive of Abdعبد, small servant, servant of lower rank
Ubaidah	عبيدة	servant of God
Ubaydullah	عبيد الله	lowly servant of Allah

Ula	علی	high rank, prestige, glory
Umar	عمر	the meaning of 'Umar' is linked with 'Aamir', prosperous, full of life, large, substantial
Umarah	عمارة	an old Arabic name
Umdah	عمدة	support
Umdatuddawlah	عمدة الدولة	support of the state
Uqba	عقبة	name of an illustrious *sahabi*. i.e. companion of the Prophet Muhammad
Urwah	عروة	Name of A Prominent *sahabi*.i.e. companion of the Prophet Muhammad
Usaid	اسید	small lion, diminutive form of Asad
Usama	اسامة	lion. Name of well-known *shaabi*. i.e. companion of the Prophet Muhammad
Uthman	عثمان	the young of a lark, a beautiful pen, name of the third Caliph of Islam.
Uzayr	عزیر	a Prophet, the biblical Ezra.

W

Wahid	واحد	one, unique, matchless. Al-Wahidالواحد, the One: one of the names of Allah
Abdul Wahid	عبدالواحد	servant of the One i.e. Allah
Wasiq	واثق	confident, sure, certain
Wadi'	ودیع	calm, peaceful

Wadood	ودود	lover, warm-hearted, affectionate, friend, beloved. Al-Wadood الودود, the All-loving: one of the names of Allah
Abdul Wadood	عبد الودود	servant of the All-loving i.e. Allah
Wafai	وفائى	associated with faithfulness, fidelity, loyalty, faith
Wafi	وفى	true, trustworthy, reliable, perfect, complete
Wafiq	وفيق	companion, friend, successful
Wahab	وهب	gift, grant, donation
Wahhab	وهّاب	donor, grantor. Al-Wahhab الوهاب, the All-giver: one of the names of Allah
Abdul Wahhab	عبد الوهاب	servant of the All-giver i.e. Allah
Wahid	وحيد	unique, matchless, singular, unparalleled
Wahiduddin	وحيد الدين	unique (manifestation) of the religion (Islam)
Wahiduzzaman	وحيد الزمان	unique (person) of the age
Wahhaj	وهّاج	shining, illuminated
Wail	وائل	coming back (for shelter)
Waiz	واعظ	admonisher, preacher
Wajahat	وجاهت	comely, dignity, elevated position
Wajid	واجد	finder, lover
Wajih	وجيه	noble, honoured, well-esteemed, illustrious
Wakil	وكيل	advocate, representative, counseller, attorney, agent

Wali	ولّي	prince, guardian, protector, friend, saint. Al-Waliyّ الولّی, the Protector: one of the names of Allah
Waliullah	ولی الله	friend of Allah
Walid	وليد	newborn, newborn child, nascent, new, boy, son. Name of a *sahabi*. i.e. companion of the Prophet Muhammad
Waqar	وقار	majesty, veneration, dignity, gracefulness.
Waris	وارث	heir, inheritor, successor. Al-Waris الوارث, the Inheritor: one of the names of Allah
Wasi	واسع	broad-minded, liberal, learned, capacious, ample, scholarly. Al-Wasi' الواسع, the All-embracing: one of the names of Allah
Abdul Wasi	عبد الواسع	servant of the All-embracing i.e. Allah
Wasim	وسيم	handsome, beautiful, graceful
Wasimuddin	وسيم الدين	handsome (person) of the religion (Islam)
Waseeq	وثيق	solid, strong, secure
Wazir	وزير	minister, vizier, an adviser or counsel to the king
Wilayat	ولاية	custody, guardianship

Y

| Yahya | يحیی | to live, will live. A Prophet, the biblical John, son of Prophet Zakaria |

Yamin (Heb)	يامين	blessed, auspicious
Yamin	يمين	right, right side, right hand
Yaqoob	يعقوب	a Prophet, the biblical Jacob, son of Prophet Ishaq
Yaqoot	ياقوت	ruby, sapphire, topaz
Yaqzan	يقظان	vigilant, awake, on the alert
Yar (Per)	يار	friend
Yar Muhammad	يار محمد	friend of the Prophet Muhammadﷺ
Yasar	يسار	prosperity, wealth, affluence, ease
Yasin	ياسين	the opening letters of the first verse of surat Ya Sin (36:1). An epithet of the Prophet Muhammadﷺ
Yasir	ياسر	easy, wealthy, afflulent
Yumn	يمن	happiness
Abul Yumn	ابو اليمن	father of happiness, happy
Yunus	يونس	a Prophet, the biblical Jonah
Yusri	يسرى	easy
Yusuf	يوسف	a Prophet, the biblical Joseph, son of Prophet Yaqub i.e. Jacob

Z

Zafir	ظافر	victorious, winner

Zafar	ظفر	victory, triumph
Zafeer	ظفير	of firm and resolute intention
Zahi	زاهى	beautiful, brilliant, glowing
Zahid	زاهد	devout, ascetic. One who renounces the world and is fully devoted to Allah
Zahir	ظاهر	apparent, evident, one of the attributes of Allah
Zahir	زاهر	a blooming flower, a bright and shining colour, lofty
Zaheer	زهير	blooming, shining, luminous
Zaheer	ظهير	helper, supporter, protector, patron
Zaheeruddin	ظهير الدين	helper of the religion (Islam)
Zaheeruddawlah	ظهير الدولة	helper of the religion (Islam)
Zahin	ذهين	sagacious, intelligent
Zaim	زعيم	leader, chief
Zaimuddin	زعيم الدين	leader of the religion (Islam).
Zaki	زكّى	pure, sinless, chaste
Zakiuddin	زكى الدين	pure (person) of the religion (Islam)
Zaman	زمان	time, age, era
Nuruzzaman	نور الزمان	light of the age
Shamsuzzaman	شمس الزمان	sun of the age
Zaman Shah	زمان شاه	king of the age
Zamil	زميل	companion, friend

Zamin	ضامن	one who stands surety for another, one who helps
Zamir	ضمير	heart, mind, conscience
Zamiruddin	ضمير الدين	heart of the religion (Islam)
Zarif	ظريف	elegant, witty, graceful
Zaid	زيد	Abundance, increase, increment, superabundance, addition, excess, surplus
Zaydan	زيدان	growth and increase
Zayn	زين	beautiful, pretty, beauty, grace, ornament, honour
Zainuddin	زين الدين	grace of the religion (Islam)
Zaynul Abidin	زين العابدين	ornament of the worshippers (of Allah)
Zhobin (Per)	ژوبين	kind of spear
Zia	ضياء	light, glow, illumination, splendour
Ziauddin	ضياء الدين	light of the religion i.e. Islam
Ziaul Haq	ضياء الحق	light of the Truth i.e. Allah
Ziaur Rahman	ضياء الرحمن	light of the most Gracious i.e. Allah
Zihni	ذهنى	intellectual, cerebral
Zill	ظلّ	shadow, shade
Zillullah	ظلّ الله	shadow of Allah
Zillur Rahman	ظل الرحمٰن	shadow of the Merciful i.e. Allah
Ziyad	زياد	increase, addition, surplus
Ziyada	زيادة	increase, addition, surplus, plenty

Ziyadatullah	زيادت الله	surplus bestowed by Allah
Zohoor	ظهور	appearance, ostentation
Zohoorul Bari	ظهور البارى	ostentation of the Creator i.e. Allah
Zubaid	زبيد	the diminutive of *zubd*, meaning cream, butter etc.
Zubair	زبير	diminutive of Zubrahزبرة, small piece of iron, a brave and wise person
Zufar	زفر	lion, a brave person, an army
Zuha	ضحىٰ	forenoon
Shamsuzzuha	شمس الضحىٰ	sun of the forenoon
Zuhair	زهير	small flower
Zuhoor	ظهور	fame, splendour, emergence
Zuka	ذُكا	the sun, dawn, morning
Zukauddin	ذُكاء الدين	sun of the religion (Islam)
Zukaullah	ذُكاء الله	sun of Allah
Zukaur Rahman	ذُكاء الرحمٰن	sun of Rahman i.e. Allah
Zulfaqar	ذوالفقار	the cleaver of vertebrae. Name of a sword presented to Ali (RA) by Muhammad
Zul-Kifl	ذوالكفل	a Prophet of Allah
Zul Qarnayn	ذو القرنين	"owner of the two horns" i.e. world conqueror, epithet of a just king mentioned in the Quran
Zunnoon	ذوالنون	(zu-al-noon) 'Lord of the fish', an epithet of Prophet Yunus i.e. Jonah who was swallowed by a big fish and later rescued by the grace of Allah

Female Names

A

Aaida	عائدة	visiting, returning
Aala	آلاء	pl. of إلى, benefit, favour, blessing
Alam	عالم	world; sing. of 'Alameen عالمين
Alam Ara (Per)	عالم آراء	adorning the world
Alima	عالمة	woman of learning, scholar
Aliya	عالية	high, tall, towering, lofty, exalted, high-ranking, sublime, superior, excellent; fem. of Aali عالى.
Aamina	آمنة	mother of the Prophet Muhammad ﷺ
Aamira	عامرة	prosperous, full of life, large, substantial; fem. of 'Aamir
Aqila	عاقلة	wise, judicious, intelligent, prudent; fem. of Aqil
Arifa	عارفة	learned, expert, authority; fem. of Arif
Abdah	عبدة	worshipper (of Allah)
Abida	عابدة	worshipper, devotee, adorer, devout; fem. of Abid
Abeer	عبير	fragrance, aroma, scent, perfume composed of musk, sandal-wood, and rose-water
Abla	عبلة	well-rounded, perfectly formed, a woman possessing a beautiful figure
Adala	عدالة	justice
Adiba	أديبة	polite, well-mannered, well-bred, courteous, polished, writer; fem. of Adib.

Adila	عديلة	equal
Adila	عادلة	honest, upright, just, righteous; fem. of Adil عادل
Afaf	عفاف	chastity, purity, honesty, righteousness, modesty, decency
Afia	عافية	good health, vigour, vitality
Afifa	عفيفة	pure, chaste, modest, virtuous, honest, righteous, upright, decent; fem. of Afif
Afkar	أفكار	pl. of Fikrفكر, intellect, thought
Afnan	أفنان	pl. of Fananفنن, branch, twig
Afra	عفراء	dust coloured, earth-coloured, a variety buck
Afrah	أفراح	pl. of Farahفرح, joy, happiness
Afrin (Per)	آفرين	praise, lucky
Afroz (Per)	افروز	illuminated
Afroza (Per)	افروزا	burning, polishing
Afsana (Per)	افسانه	fable, fiction, romance
Afsar (Per)	افسر	crown
Afsar Ara (Per)	افسر آرا	adorning the crown
Afza (Per)	افزا	increase, augmentation
Agharid	اغاريد	pl. of Ughrudah أغرودة, twittering, song
Aghsan	أغصان	pl. of Ghusnغصن, branch, twig
Ahd	عهد	pledge, knowledge
Ahdaf	أهداف	pl. of Hadafهدف, aim, goal, target
Ahlam	احلام	pl. of Hulm حلم, dream

Ayesha	عائشة	living, well-off, well-to-do, prosperous. Aisha (d. 678): wife of the Prophet Muhammadﷺ and daughter of Khalifa Abu Bakr
Akhtar (Per)	اختر	star, good luck
Akida	اكيدة	certain, firm
Akifa	عاكفة	devoted to, dedicated to, intent, busy; fem. of Akif
Alhan	ألحان	melody
Alifa	أليفة	friendly, sociable, amicable; fem. of Alif
Aleema	عليمة	exalted, highest social standing
Aliya	عليّة	highest social standing, lofty, sublime; fem. of Ali
Almasa	ألماسة	diamond
Altaf	الطاف	pl. of Lutfلطف, kindness
Alya	علياء	heaven (s), sky, sublimity, lofty
Aamal	آمال	pl. of Amalأمل, hope, expectation, aspirations
Amal	أمل	hope, expectation; sing. of Amaalآمال
Aman	أمان	trust, safety, protection, tranquillity, peace of mind, calmness
Amanat	أمانات	pl. of Amanah أمانت, trust, deposit
Amani	أمانى	wishes, aspirations, hopes; pl. of Umniyah أمنية
Ama	أمة	female slave, servant
Amatul Islam	أمة الاسلام	(female) servant of Islam
Amatul Karim	أمة الكريم	(female) servant of the most generous i.e. Allah

Amatullah	أمة الله	(female) servant of Allah
Ambara	عنبرة	perfume, ambergris; fem. of Ambar
Ambarin (Per)	عنبرين	perfumed
Ameera	أميرة	princess; fem. of Ameer. See Ameer (m.)
Amila	آملة	hopeful
Amina	آمنة	safe, secure, protected, a lady of peace and harmony. Name of the beloved mother of the Prophet Muhammad
Amira	عامرة	an occupant of an abode, one who makes umrah or ziyaarah, abundant treasure
Amina	أمينة	trustworthy, faithful, honest; fem. of Amin أمين.
Amjad	أمجاد	pl. of Majd مجد, glory, honour
Ammara	عمّاره	a lady with strong *Imaan;* tolerant
Amna	أمنة	safety
Amra	عمرة	any covering for the head, as a crown
Anadil	عنادل	pl. of Andalib عندليب, nightingale
Anan	عنان	clouds
Anat	اناة	perseverance, patience
Anbar (ambar)	عنبر	perfume, ambergiris
Andalah	عندلة	song of the nightingale
Andalib	عندليب	nightingale; sing. of Anadil عنادل
Anisa	آنسة	a pious-hearted lady, good-natured, compatible
Anisa	أنيسة	companion, affectionate, friendly, sociable, intimate friend; fem. of Anis
Aniqa	أنيقة	neat, elegant, smart

Anjum	انجم	pl. Najmنجم, star
Anjuman (Per)	انجمن	assembly
Anjuman Ara (per)	انجمن آرا	adorning the assembly
Ansam	أنسام	pl. of Nasamنسم, breath, breath of life
Anwar	أنوار	rays of light; pl. of Noor نور
Aqiba	عاقبة	result, consequence
Aqila	عاقلة	wise, sensible, intelligent, sensible, discerning
Aqeela	عقيلة	the best, the very best
Ara (Per)	آرا	adorning
Husn Ara (Ar-Per)	حسن آرا	adorning the beauty
Jahan Ara (Per)	جهان آرا	adorning the world
Areefa	عريفة	learned, expert, authority; fem. of Areefعريف.
Areej/Arij	أريج	fragrance, aroma, sweet smell, scent, perfume
Arjumand (Per)	أرجمند	excellent, beloved, noble
Arjumand Bano	أرجمند بانو	excellent woman, noble woman
Arzu (Per)	آرزو	wish, hope, love
Asar	آثار	pl. of Asar الر, sign, mark, trace.
Ashraf	أشرف	nobler, more honourable; comp. adj. of Sharifشريف.
Ashwaq	أشواق	pl. of Shawqشوق, longing, desire, wish
Asila	اثيلة	highborn, of noble origin
Asila	أصيلة	of noble origin, highborn, pure; fem. of Asil أصيل.

Asima	عاصمة	safe, chaste, protector, guardian; fem. of Asim
Asira	أثيرة	honoured, chosen, preferred; fem. of Asir
Asira	آصرة	bond
Asiya	آسية	comforting, consoling, a mansion with solid foundation or pillars, firm, powerful. Wife of Fir'awn.
Asma	أسماء	higher, more exalted, more sublime, more eminent
Asmaa	أسماء	pl. of Ism اسم, name
'Asmaa	عصماء	chaste, virtuous, precious, valuable, excellent
Asra	أسرىٰ	to travel by night, to make someone travel by night
Atifa	عاطفة	compassion, affection, sympathetic, kindness; fem. of Atif
Atifa	عطيفة	affectionate, compassionate
Atika	عاتكة	clear, pure, limpid (of wine)
Atiqa	عاتقة	emancipated, a beautiful lady
Atiqa	عتيقة	ancient, noble; fem. of Atiq
Atira	عاطرة	fragrant, connoisseur of good fragrance, aromatic, perfumed
Atiya	عطيّة	gift, present, bounty, grant
Atuf	عطوف	affectionate, kind hearted, compassionate, loving
Awatif	عواطف	pl. of Aatifa عاطفة, affection, compassion, kindness, kind feeling
Ayn	عين	source, spring
Aynun Nahr	عين النهر	source of the spring

Azhar	أزهار	pl. of Zahrah زهرة, flower, blossom.
Azima	عظيمة	great, powerful, dignified, magnificent, glorious; fem. of Azim
Azima	عزيمة	determination, firm will
Aziza	عزيزة	noble, precious, cherished, honourable, illustrious, highly esteemed, dearly loved, beloved; fem., of Aziz
Azra	عذراء	virgin, maiden, a young unmarried lady
Azwa	أضواء	pl. of Zau ضوء, light, splendour, limelight

B

Baria	بارعة	excelling, originator; fem. of Bari
Badai	بدائع	pl. of Badia بديعة, wonder, marvel
Badiha	بديهة	insight, perceptive faculty
Badr	بدر	full moon of the fourteenth night
Badrun Nisa	بدر النساء	full moon of the women
Badriyah	بدرية	full moon-like
Baha	بهاء	beauty, glory, splendour, magnificence, glow
Bahar (Per)	بهار	spring, blossom
Bahar banu (Per)	بهار بانو	blooming princess
Bahija	بهيجة	glad, happy, joyful, delighted, delightful, cheerful; fem. of Bahij
Bahira	باهرة	brilliant, superb, magnificent, gorgeous, spectacular
Bahira	بهيرة	dazzling, brilliant

Bahiya	بهيَّة	beautiful, brilliant, elegant, radiant, pretty, charming; fem. of Bahi
Bahjat	بهجت	splendour, magnificence, pomp, joy, happiness
Baiza	بيضاء	white, bright, brilliant, innocent, pure; fem. of Abyad
Bajila	بجيلة	honoured, dignified, highly regarded
Bakarah	بكارة	virginity
Bakura	بكورة	coming early
Bakhita	بخيتة	lucky, fortunate; fem. of Bakhit
Balqis	بلقيس	queen of Saba popularly pronounced as Bilqis
Baligha	بليغة	eloquent
Banan	بنان	fingertips
Banafsaj	بنفسج	violet flower
Banu (Per)	بانو	princess, lady, Miss
Baraim	براعم	pl. of Burum برعم, blossom, bud
Barakat	بركت	blessing; sing. of Barakat بركات
Barat	براءة	innocence, guiltlessness
Bari'a	بريئة	innocent, blameless, guiltless, sound; fem. of Bari'
Barraqa	برّاقة	bright, brilliant, shining, sparkling, glittering; fem. of Barraq
Basharat	بشارت	good news, glad tidings
Bashira	بشيرة	bringer of good news; fem. of Bashir, harbinger
Basila	باسلة	brave, fearless, intrepid
Basima	باسمة	smiling; fem. of Basim

Basira	بصيرة	sagacious, endowed with insight; fem. of Basir. See Basir (m.)
Basma	بسمة	smile
Bassama	بسّامة	smiling; fem. of Bassam
Batul	بتول	virgin, pure and chaste, maiden. A lady who is purely devoted to Allah, an epithet of Maryam, mother of Prophet 'Isa (Jesus), and of Fatima, daughter of the Prophet Muhammadﷺ
Begam/Begum (Per)	بیگم	honorific title, queen, lady of rank
Benazir (Per)	بینظیر	matchless, unique
Bibi (Per)	بی بی	lady of rank, and honorific title used at the end of a woman's name in the Indian sub-continent
Bilqis	بلقیس	queen of Saba known as Bilqis in the Arabian tradition
Budur	بدور	pl. of Badrبدر, full moon.
Bulbul	بلبل	nightingale
Burum	برعم	bud, blossom; sing. of Baraim براعم.
Busaina	بثينة	diminutive of Basna بثنة, beautiful woman
Bushra	بشرىٰ	good news, glad tidings
Bustan	بستان	garden, orchard

D

Daiba	دائبة	assiduous, persistent, devoted
Dalal	دلال	coquetry, pampering
Dalia	دالیا	Dahlia, flower
Danish	دانش	wisdom, learning

Danish Ara	دانش آرا	endowed with wisdom, learning
Dara	دارة	halo (of the moon)
Daria	دارية	learned, knowing
Daulat	دولة	wealth, empire, state, power
Dawha	دوحة	lofty tree with many branches, family tree
Dil (Per)	دل	heart, mind
Dilara (Per)	دل آرا	beloved, one who decorates heart
Dildar (Per)	دلدار	having a big heart. Wife of Mughal emperor Babur
Dilruba (Per)	دلربا	heart-ravishing, a beloved object
Dilshad (Per)	دلشاد	happy, glad, cheerful
Dima	ديمة	An incessant gentle rain unaccompanied by wind, thunder, or lightning
Doha	ضحیٰ	forenoon
Dunya	دنيا	world, earth
Durr	در	pearls
Durrah	درّة	pearl. A sahabia i.e. a muslim woman who lived in time of Prophet Muhammad ﷺ
Durriya	درية	glittering, sparkling, twinkling, brilliant

F

Faiza	فائزه	victorious, triumphant, winner, successful, prosperous; fem. of Faiz
Fakhira	فاخرة	excellent, glorious, magnificent, precious, honourable
Fariha	فارحة	happy, glad, delighted, cheerful, joyful; fem. of Farih

Fatin	فاتن	beautiful, pretty, attractive, glamorous, captivating, ravishing
Fatina	فاتنة	fem. of Fatin
Fadia	فادية	redeemer, ransomer; fem. of Fadi
Fadwa	فدوى	name derived from self-sacrifice
Faheema	فهيمة	intelligent, judicious, learned, erudite; fem. of Faheem
Fahhama	فهامة	very intelligent, learned, very understanding
Fahm	فهم	intellect, intelligence, insight
Fahm Ara (Per)	فهم آرا	adorned with intellect, intelligent
Fahmida (Per)	فهميدة	intelligent, judicious
Faida	فائدة	benefit, advantage, gain, worth, welfare
Faiqa	فائقة	excellent, outstanding, distinguished, superior, ascendant
Fajr	فجر	dawn, rise, beginning, start
Fakhar	فخار	honour, pride, glory
Fakhr	فخر	glory, pride, honour
Fakhrun Nisa	فخر النساء	glory of the women
Fakhriya	فخرية	proud, honorary, glory, pride (for noble cause); fem. of Fakhri
Falak	فلك	orbit, sky, celestial sphere
Faliha	فالحة	fortunate, lucky, successful, prosperous; fem. of Falih
Faqiha	فقيهة	jurist, expert, scholar in fiqh (Islamic jusrisprudence); fem. of Faqih
Farah	فرح	joy, happiness, cheerfulness, delight
Farha	فرحة	gladness, pleasure, happiness, delight

Farhana	فرحانة	glad, joyful, happy, cheerful, delighted; fem. of Farhan
Farhi	فرحى	glad, happy
Faria	فارعة	tall, towering, lofty, pretty, slim, slender, fem. of Fari
Farida	فريدة	unique, matchless, singular, precious; fem. of Farid
Fariha	فريحة	happy, glad, joyful
Farwa	فروة	fur; (daughter of Imam Ja'far al-Sadiq)
Faryal (Tur)	فريال	name
Farzana (Per)	فرزانه	wise, learned
Fasiha	فصيحة	eloquent, fluent, well-spoken; fem. of Fasih
Fathiya	فتحية	one who wins victory after victory; fem. of Fathi
Fatiha	فاتحة	opening, introduction, dawn, first
Fatima	فاطمة	literally: weaner, daughter of Muhammadﷺ and wife of Khalifa Ali known as Sayyidat-al-Nisa (the chief of women)
Fatinah	فاتنة	charming, fascinating, alluring, captivating
Fattanan	فتّانة	extremely beautiful, charming, captivating
Fawha	فوحة	breath of fragrance
Fawza	فوزة	victory, triumph, success, winning, achievement
Fawziya	فوزيّة	triumphant, successful, victorious, fem. of Fawzi
Fayrooz	فيروز	turquoise
Fayyaza	فياضة	a lady who confers great favours, most generous and bountiful

Fazila	فاضلة	virtuous, honest, excellent, superior, kind, outstanding, eminent, learned; fem. of Fazil (fadil)
Fazila	فضيلة	high degree of excellence, merit, perfection, outstanding, virtue, excellence, knowledge
Fazilatun Nisa	فضيلة النساء	excellence of the women
Fidda	فضة	silver
Firdaus	فردوس	paradise, heaven, garden
Firdausi	فردوسى	heavenly
Fairuza	فيروزة	turquoise, a bright greenish-blue coloured precious stone
Fuada	فؤادة	heart; fem. of fuad
Funoon	فنون	variety, art
Furoozan	فروزان	luminous, radiant

G

Ghania	غانية	beauty, beautiful girl, pretty girl, danseuse
Ghada	غادة	delicate young girl, beautiful young woman, youthful and beautiful woman
Ghadeer	غدير	brook, rivulet, small stream
Ghaida	غيداء	young and delicate, soft
Ghalia	غالية	precious, priceless, valuable, dear, beloved
Ghaliba	غالبة	conqueror, victor, winner; fem. of Ghalib غالب.
Ghaniya	غنيَّة	rich, wealthy, prosperous; fem. of Ghani.
Ghazal	غزال	gazelle, deer

Ghazala	غزالة	gazelle, a young deer, the sun
Ghina	غناء	singing, song
Ghufran	غفران	pardon, forgiveness
Ghusn	غصن	branch, twig; sing. of Ghusoon غصون.
Ghusun	غصون	pl. of Ghusn غصن, branch, twig
Gul (Per)	گل	flower, rose
Gul Badan (Per)	گلبدن	beautiful body resembling rose
Gul Bahar (Per)	گل بهار	rose spring
Gul Barg (Per)	گلبرك	rose petal
Gulistan (Per)	گلستان	rose garden, garden
Gul-izar (Per)	گل عذار	rosy-cheeked
Gul Rana (Per)	گل رعنا	beautiful delicate scented rose
Gul Rang(Per)	گل رنگ	rose-coloured
Gul-ru (Per)	گل رو	rosy-faced
Gul Rukh (Per)	گل رخ	rose-face
Gulshan (Per)	گلشن	rose-garden
Gulzaar (Per)	گلزار	rose-garden
Gulab (Per)	گلاب	rose, rosewater

H

Hafiza	حافظة	honorific title of a woman who has memorised the Quran, guardian, protector; fem. Hafiz
Halima	حالمة	dreamer, visionary
Hamida	حامدة	praiser (of Allah); fem. of Hamid

Harisa	حارثة	cultivator, lioness; fem. of Haris (Harith)
Harisa	حارسة	guard, protector (f.)
Habiba	حبيبة	beloved, darling, sweetheart; fem. of Habib
Hadaya	هدايا	pl. of Hadiyaهديّة, gift, present
Hadia	هادية	guide to righteousness; fem. of Hadi هادى leader
Hadeel	هديل	cooing of a pigeon.
Hadiya	هديّة	gift, present; sing. of Hadayaهدايا.
Haffafa	هفّافة	glittering, shining, thin, peaceful, gentle wind
Hafeeza	حفيظة	guardian, protector; fem. of Hafeezحفيظ.
Hafsa	حفصة	cub; wife of Muhammadﷺ; daughter of Khalifa 'Umar
Hajara	هاجرة	Wife of Prophet Ibrahim and mother ofProphet Ismail
Hakeema	حكيمة	wise, sage, judicious, prudent; fem. of Hakeem. A sahabia i.e. a muslim woman who lived in time of the Prophet Muhammadﷺ
Hala	هالة	halo, ring around the eye, aureole, name of the sister of Khadija, the first wife of the Prophet Muhammadﷺ
Halima	حليمة	clement, patient, tolerant, gentle; fem. of Halim. Halima al-Sadiyah: foster mother of the Prophet Muhammadﷺ
Hamama	حمامة	dove, pigeon
Hamda	حمدة	praise, laudation of Allah; fem. of Hamd.
Hammada	حمادة	praising (God)
Hamdan	حمدان	much praise. A tribe in Arabia

Hamida	حميدة	praised, commended, praiseworthy, commendable; fem. of Hamid
Hamima	حميمة	close friend
Hana	هناء	happiness, bliss, felicity
Hanan	حنان	compassion, affection, love, mercy, tenderness, warm-heartedness
Hanifa	حنيفة	true, one of true faith, upright; fem. of Hanif
Hania	هائنة	happy, delighted
Hanin	حنين	desire, longing, yearning
Haniya	هنيَّة	pleasant, happy
Hanna	حنَّة	compassion, sympathy, pity
Hanoon	حنون	compassionate, merciful, affectionate, tender-hearted, soft-hearted
Hanoona	حنونة	compassionate; fem. of Hanun
Hareer	حرير	silk
Hasana	حسنة	good deed, kind act, favour; sing. of Hasanat
Hasiba	حسيبة	highborn, respected, noble; fem. of Hasib
Hasifa	حصيفة	judicious, wise, prudent, sagacious, endowed with sound judgment; fem. of Hasif
Hasina	حسينة	pretty, beautiful
Hasina	حصينة	well-fortified, guarded, chaste, virtuous
Hasna	حسناء	pious, beautiful woman
Hasna	حصناء	chaste, virtuous, modest

Hassana	حسّانة	most beautiful woman, most sweetheart
Hawwa	حواء	a beautiful girl with a ruddy complexion, Eve; wife of Adam, mother of mankind
Haya'	حياء	shyness, bashfulness, coyness, modesty
Hayat	حيات	life
Aynul Hayat	عين الحياة	fountain of life
Hayfa	هيفاء	slender, slim, of beautiful body
Hazar	هزار	kind of nightingale
Hazima	حازمة	firm, energetic, judicious, discreet, prudent; fem. of Hazim
Hiba	هبة	gift, present
Hibatullah	هبة الله	gift of God
Hikmat	حكمت	wisdom
Hilal	هلال	crescent, new moon
Hind	هند	proper name
Hana	هناء	happiness, bliss
Hashmat	حشمت	modesty, bashfulness, decency, decorum
Hiyam	هيام	passionate love
Hoyam	هيام	passionate love
Huda	هدىٰ	right guidance, right path
Humaida	حميدة	praised; fem. of Humaid
Humayra	حميراء	of red colour. Name of Ayesha, wife of the Prophet Muhammad ﷺ
Hooriya	حورية	Virgin of Paradise, houri, nymph
Hurriya	حرية	freedom, liberty
Husaina	حسينة	diminutive of Husn حسن, beauty

Hushaima	حشيمة	diminutive of Hishma حشمت, modesty
Husn	حسن	beauty, gracefulness, prettiness
Husne Ara (Per. Ar.) حسن آرا		adorned with beauty
Husna	حسنىٰ	most pious, good outcome; fem. of Ahsan أحسن.
Husni	حسنى	possessing beauty
Huzuz	حظوظ	pl. of Hazz حظ, fortune, good luck

I

Iba	إباء	pride, disdain
Ibriz	إبريز	pure gold
Ibrisam	ابريسام	silk
Ibrisami	ابريسمى	silken
Ibtihaj	ابتهاج	joy, delight
Ibtihal	ابتهال	prayer, supplication
Ibtisam	ابتسام	smile
Ibtisama	ابتسامة	smile
Idrak	ادراك	intellect, perception, achievement, attainment
Iffat	عفّت	purity, chastity, modesty, virtue, abstinence
Iftikhar	افتخار	pride
Iftinan	افتنان	enchantment, captivation
Ihtisham	احتشام	chastity, modesty, decency, decorum
Ijlal	إجلال	glorification, exaltation, honour, distinction, respect

Ikhlas	إخلاص	sincerity, honesty, integrity, fidelity, faithfulness
Iklil	إكليل	crown, garland, wreath
Ikram	اكرام	honour, glory, respect, generosity, hospitality
Ilham	الهام	intuition, inspiration, revelation
Iltimas	التماس	request, appeal, entreaty
Ilyas (Heb)	الياس	name of a Prophet of Allah. He was called Ilyaseen as well
Iman	إيمان	belief, faith in Allah
Imtinan	امتنان	gratitude, gratefulness, thankfulness
Imtisal	امتثال	obedience, conforming to, in compliance with
Imtiyaz	امتياز	distinction, mark of honour, intelligent
Inam	انعام	gift, present, act of kindness, benefaction, bestowal
Inas	إيناس	friendliness, cordiality, sociability
Inayat	عنايت	concern, solicitude
Inshirah	إنشراح	joy, delight, happiness, cheerfulness
Intisar	انتصار	victory, triumph; sing
Intisarat	انتصارات	pl. of Intisar انتصار, victory, triumph
Iradat	إرادت	wish, desire, intention
Irtiza	ارتضاء	contentment, approval
Isad	إسعاد	making happy or prosperous, blessing
Ishraq	إشراق	brilliance, radiance, shining
Ishrat	عشرت	pleasure, enjoyment, delight

Islah	إصلاح	making right, making good, improvement, betterment
Ismat	عصمت	purity, honour, protection, chastity, modesty
Istabraq	إستبرق	brocade
Itidal	اعتدال	moderateness, moderation, mildness, rectitude
Itimad	اعتماد	reliance, dependence
Izaz	إعزاز	honour, esteem, regard, affection
Izdihar	إزدهار	prosperity, flourishing, bloom, blossoming
Izza	عزة	honour, fame, power

J

Jaan (Per)	جان	life
Jaanaan (Per)	جانان	pretty, sweet-heart; pl. of Jan جان, life
Jabin	جبين	forehead
Jadida	جديدة	new, fresh
Jahan (Per)	جهان	world
Ashraf Jahan (Ar.Per)	أشرف جهان	noblest of the world
Jahan Ara (Per)	جهان آرا	adorning the world. Daughter of Mughal emperor Shah Jahaan
Khurshid Jahan (Per)	خورشيد جهان	sun of the world
Noor Jahan (Ar. Per.)	نورجهان	light of the world
Raunaq Jahan (Ar. Per)	رونق جهان	lustre of the world

Jala	جلاء	bringing to light, shining, clarity, elucidation
Jalila	جليلة	great, exalted, magnificent; fem. of Jalil
Jamia	جامعة	gatherer, collector, author, writer; fem. of Jami جامع.
Jamila	جميلة	beautiful, elegant, pretty; fem. of Jamil. Daughter of Khalifa Umar
Janan	جنان	heart, soul, pretty
Janna	جنة	garden, paradise
Jannatul Firdaus	جنة الفردوس	Garden of Paradise
Jawda	جودة	excellence, high, quality, fineness
Jawhara	جوهرة	jewel, gem, essence
Jawahir	جواهر	precious
Jazibiyya	جاذبية	attraction, charm, appeal
Jibla	جبلة	nature, natural disposition
Jinan	جنان	pl. of Jannatجنة, garden, paradise
Jumaina	جمينة	diminutive of Jumanaجمانة, small pearl
Jumana	جمانة	pearl
Junna	جنة	shelter
Junayna	جنينة	little garden
Juwairiyah	جويريّة	diminutive of Jooriyah جوريّة, damask rose. Wife of the Prophet Muhammadﷺ

K

Kabira	كبيرة	great

Kakuli (Per)	كاكلى	crest, tuft on the head of an animal like comb of a cock
Kamila	كاملة	perfect, complete, genuine; fem. of kamil
Kaniz	كنيز	maid servant, female servant, virgin
Karam	كرم	generosity, bounty, noble nature
Karima	كريمة	kind, generous, benevolent, open-handed, bountiful, noble; fem. of Karim
Karma	كرمة	vine, grapevine, kind, generous
Kausar	كوثر	abundance, name of a fountain in the paradise
Kawkab	كوكب	star, satellite
Kazima	كاظمة	one who controls or suppresses her anger; fem. of Kazim
Khadija	خديجة	the first wife of the Prophet Muhammad ﷺ who was the first to embrace Islam
Khadra	خضراء	green, verdant
Khalida	خالدة	permanent, immortal, eternal; fem. of Khalid
Khalisa	خالصة	pure, true, clear, real; fem. of Khalis
Khansa	خنساء	proper name (famous Arabic poetess), pugnosed
Khanum/Khanam	خانم	princess, noble woman
Khashia	خاشعة	pious, devout; fem. of Khashi
Khasiba	خصيبة	fruitful, fertile, prolific, prodigal, productive; fem. of Khasib
Khatiba	خطيبة	orator, speaker, fiancee

Khatira	خاطرة	wish, desire
Khaula	خولة	a buck, deer, name of a well-known *sahabi* i.e. companion of the Prophet Muhammadﷺ
Khatoon (Per)	خاتون	noblewoman, lady
Khair	خير	good, blessing, boon, wealth, fortune
Khairun Nisa	خير النساء	best of women. Epithet of Khadija, the first wife of the Prophet Muhammadﷺ
Khaira	خيرة	the best, prime, top, flower, cream; sing. of Khairat خيرات.
Khairat	خيرات	pl. of Khaira خيرة, blessing, good work
Khairiya	خيريّة	charity, benevolence, beneficence, good
Khudra	خضرة	greenery, greenness, verdancy
Khulud	خلود	immortality
Khursheed	خورشيد	sun
Khursheed Jahan	خورشيد جهان	sun of the world
Khuzama	خزامىٰ	lavender, tulip
Kishwar (Per)	كشور	country
Kohinoor	كوه نور	the mountain of light, name of a diamond that was a prized possession of the Mughals
Kubra	كبرىٰ	great, senior, (al-Kubra–epithet of Khadija)
Kulsoom	كلثوم	full of flesh about the face and cheeks, rosy, healthy cheeks, chubby cheeks
Umm Kulsoom	ام كلثوم	daughter of Muhammadﷺ married to Khalifa Usman (*Uthman*)

L

Labiba	لبيبة	intelligent, judicious, sensible, understanding, sagacious, wise, prudent, wise; fem. of Labib
Laiqa	لائقة	worthy, deserving, elegant, capable, decent
Lama/Luma/Lima	لمى	darkness of inner lips, it is considered to be beautiful
Lamia	لامعة	brilliant, lustrous, shining, radiant
Lamisa	لميسة	soft to touch
Lamya	لمياء	dark-lipped (from inside)
Latifa	لطيفة	pretty, charming, gentle, sweet, refined, kind, pleasantry, humour, friendly; fem. of Latif
Layaan	ليان	gentleness, softness, tenderness
Layla	ليلىٰ	a well-known character in Arabic literature i.e. the beloved of Majnoon
Layina	لينة	tender, supple, resilient
Lina	لينة	gentle, soft, tender, 'a kind of palm'
Lubaba	لبابة	essence, core, gist
Lubana	لبانة	wish, desire
lubna	لبنىٰ	a tree which yields an aromatic resin used in perfume and medicine i.e. storax-tree
Lulu	لؤلؤ	pearls
Lulua	لؤلؤة	pearl

Lutf	لطف	kindness, friendliness, courtesy, delicate, grace, favour from Allah
Lutfun Nisa	لطف النساء	grace of women
Lutfiya	لطفية	delicate, graceful

M

Maisa	مائسة	walking with a proud gait
Majida	ماجدة	glorious, noble, honourable, generous; fem. of Majid
Mas	ماس	for Almas الماس: diamond. (only almas is used as name)
Mabrooka	مبروكة	blessed, prosperous, abundant; fem. of Mabrook
Madaniya	مدنية	civilized, urbane, polished
Madiha	مديحة	praiseworthy, commendation, commendable
Mah (Per)	ماه	moon
Mah Jabin (Per)	ماه جبين	(maah jabeen): (beautiful) brow like the moon
Mah Liqa (Per.Ar.)	ماه لقا	moon-like (face)
Mah Naz (Per)	ماه ناز	humble moon (that would disappear on touch)
Mah Nur (Per)	ماه نور	moonlight
Mah Rukh (Per)	ماه رخ	face as bright as the moon
Mahtab(Per)	ماهتاب	moonlight
Maha	مها	wild cow (representing beauty)
Mahabbat/Muhabbat	محبت	love, affection

Mahasin	محاسن	pl. of Mahsana محسنة, beauty, charm, charming, attraction, virtue, merit
Mahbooba	محبوبة	dear, beloved sweetheart; fem. of Mahboob
Mahdiya	مهدية	rightly guided; fem. of Mahdi. see Rashidaرشيدة, rightly guided
Mahfooza	محفوظة	safeguarded, well-protected; fem. of Mahfooz
Mahira	ماهرة	skilled, skilful, proficient; fem. of Mahir
Mahjooba	محجوبة	hidden, covered, screened; fem. of Mahjoob
Mahmooda	محمودة	praised, praiseworthy, elegant, lauded
Mahmoodatun Nisa محمودة النساء		praised (one) of the women
Maimana	ميمنة	right, right-hand side, right wing (of army)
Maisara	ميسرة	prosperity, abundance, wealth, effluence, ; left, left-hand side, left wing (of army)
Maisoora	ميسورة	ease; successful, fortunate, lucky, prosperous; fem. of Maisoor
Majda	مجدة	glory, honour, nobility
Majdiya	مجدية	glorious
Majida	ماجدة	glorious, noble, respected, exalted, fem. of Majidماجد.
Majeeda	مجيدة	glorious, noble, sublime, exalted; fem. of Majeedمجيد.
Makarim	مكارم	of good and honourable character
Malaha	ملاحة	beauty, grace, elegance
Malaika	ملائكة	angels
Malak	ملك	angel

Maliha	مليحة	beautiful, pretty, good-looking; fem. of Malih مليح.
Malika	مالكة	reigning, ruling
Maleeka	مليكة	queen; fem. of Maleek مليك.
Malika	ملكة	fem. of Malik ملك: queen
Mamoona	مأمونة	trustworthy, honest, faithful, reliable; fem. of mamoon
Manahil	مناهل	pl. of Manhal منهل, spring, of salubrious water, fountain
Manal	منال	attainment, achievement, acquisition
Manar	منار	guiding light, light-house
Manara	منارة	fem. of Manar: light-house
Mann	منّ	gift, present, favour, benefit, boon
Mannana	منانة	bountiful, generous; fem. of Mannan
Mansoora	منصورة	assisted, victorious, supported, trumphant; fem. of Mansoor
Manzoora	منظورة	approved of, chosen, promising; fem. of Manzoor
Maqboola	مقبولة	accepted, admitted, granted, approved; fem. of Maqbool
Maqsooda	مقصودة	intended, destined
Marab	مأرب	wish, desire, purpose, use, aim; sing. of Marib مآرب.
Maram	مرام	wish, desire, aspiration
Maria	مارية	a lady with fair complexion, kind of bird. Wife of Muhammadﷺ who gave birth to son named Ibrahim

Marib	مآرب	pl. of ma'rab مأرب, wish
Marjan	مرجان	small pearls, corals
Maroofa	معروفة	famous, known, eminent, kindness, kind act; fem. of Maruf
Marwa	مروة	flint-stone
Mariam	مريم	mother of the Prophet 'Isa (Jesus), the Biblical Mary
Marziya	مرضيّة	accepted, well-pleased, one who is pleasing
Marzooqa	مرزوقة	blessed, fortunate, prosperous, successful; fem. of Marzooq
Mariha	مرحة	joyful, cheerful, lively
Marghuba	مرغوبة	coveted, desired
Masabih	مصابيح	pl. of Misbah مصباح, lamp
Masarrat	مسرت	joy, delight, pleasure, gladness, happiness
Mashhuda	مشهودة	present, manifest
Mashia	مشيئة	wish, desire, will (of Allah)
Masrurah	مسرورة	glad, happy, delighted
Mastura	مستورة	latent, hidden, chaste
Masooda	مسعودة	fortunate, happy, lucky, prosperous, gracious, favourable, august; fem. of Masood
Masooma	معصومة	innocent, sinless, safe-guarded, protected; fem. of Masoom
Masoon	مصون	safeguarded, well-protected
Matina	متينة	strong, solid, of resolute mind
Mawadda	مودّة	friendship, intimacy, affection, love

Mawhiba	موهبة	gift, talent; sing. of Mawahib مواهب.
Mawhooba	موهوبة	gifted, talented, favoured; fem. of Mawhoob
Mawsoofa	موصوفة	worthy of description, portrayed, endowed with laudable qualities; fem. of Mawsoof
Maimoona	ميمونة	auspicious, prosperous, lucky, fortunate, blessed; fem. of Maimoon
Maisa	ميساء	to walk with a proud swinging gait
Maisoon	ميسون	of beautiful face and body
Mayyada	ميّادة	to walk with swinging gait
Mazida	مزيدة	increase, excess, high degree, maximum; fem. of Mazid مزيد.
Maziyah	مزيّة	excellence, merit, virtue
Mihr (Per)	مهر	sun, affection
Mehrun Nisaa (Per. Ar)مهر النساء		sun of the women
Midha	مدحت	praise, eulogy
Mahin	مهين	fine, subtle, thin. Name of a woman
Minnat	منّت	grace, kindness, favour, gift
Minoo (Per)	مينو	paradise
Misam	ميسم	impression, mark, beauty
Muazzama	معظّمة	exalted, respected, glorified; fem. of Muazzam معظّم.
Mubaraka	مباركة	blessed, fortunate, lucky, auspicious; fem. of Mubarak
Mubina	مبينة	clear, manifest, plain, distinct; fem. of Mubinمبين.

Mufida	مفيدة	beneficial, advantageous, favourable, useful, profitable
Muhayya	محيّا	countenance, face, look
Muhja	مهجة	heart, soul
Muhra	مهرة	filly, a female pony
Muhsana	محصنة	chaste, virtuous, protected, sheltered, pure, modest, married woman
Muhsina	محسنة	benevolent, beneficent, charitable, humanitarian; fem. of Muhsin
Muida	معيدة	revisor, teacher, fem. of Muid
Mujahida	مجاهدة	one who struggles, strives, or fights for the cause of Islam; fem. of Mujahid
Mujiba	مجيبة	one who answers or grants something
Mukarrama	مكرمة	honoured, reverred, honourable; fem. of Mukarram
Mukhlisa	مخلصة	devoted, faithful, pure-hearted
Mulayka	مليكة	diminutive of Malaka ملكة, angel
Mulook	ملوك	pl. of Malik ملك, king
Mumina	مؤمنة	believer (in Islam); fem. of Mumin
Mumtaz	ممتاز	distinguished, exalted, superior, outstanding
Mumtaz Mahal	ممتاز محل	wife of Mughal emperor Shah Jahan
Mumtaza	ممتازة	fem. of Mumtaz
Muna	منى	pl. of Munya منية, wish, desire
Munas Sabah	منى الصباح	wishes of the dawn

Munawwara	منوّرة	illuminated, brilliant, full of light; fem. of Munawwar.
Muniba	منيبة	one who turns towards Allah, one who repents
Munifa	منيفة	eminent, exalted, superior, high, lofty; fem. of Munif
Munira	منيرة	bright, brilliant, shedding light, radiant, luminous, shining; fem. of Munir
Munisa	مؤنسة	sociable, friendly, kind, gentle; fem. of Munis
Munya	منية	wish, desire, object of desire; sing. of Muna منى, wishes
Munyatul Muna	منية المنى	wish of wishes
Muqaddasa	مقدسة	sacred, holy
Muriha	مريحة	restful, soothing
Murshida	مرشدة	leader, guide, adviser, counsellor; fem. of Murshid
Musaddiqa	مصدقة	one who affirms the truth
Musawat	مساوات	equality
Musharrafa	مشرفة	honoured, elevated
Mushira	مشيرة	counsellor, adviser; fem. of Mushir
Mushtari	المشترى	jupiter
Muslima	مسلمة	(female) follower of the religion of Islam; fem. of Muslim
Mutahhara	مطهّرة	purified, chaste
Mutia	مطيعة	obedient, pious, devoted, faithful; fem. of Muti'

Muwaffaqa	موفّقة	successful, prosperous, lucky, fortunate; fem. of Muwaffaq
Muzaina	مزينة	diminutive of Muzna مزنة, rain clouds
Muyassar	ميسّر	successful, lucky, prosperous
Muzna	مزنة	rain clouds

N

Nabiha	نابهة	noble, famous, eminent, distinguished, brilliant; fem. of Nabih
Naima	ناعمة	delicate, soft, smooth
Naira	نائره	shining, glittering
Najia	ناجية	saved, liberated; fem. of Naji
Najiha	ناجحة	successful, prosperous; fem. of Najih
Nasia	ناصعة	clear, pure; fem. of Nasi
Nasifa	ناصفة	just, equitable
Nasiha	ناصحة	advisor, sincere
Nasira	ناصرة	helper, aide, assistant, protector
Naaz (Per)	ناز	glory, pride, elegance, gracefulness, fresh
Naziha	نازهة	pure, honest
Nazima	ناظمة	arranger, organizer, poetess; fem. of Nazim
Nazira	ناظرة	observer, supervisor
Nazira	ناضرة	one with healthy and happy looks, radiant, flourishing, resplendent, bright, beaming
Nabaha	نباهة	fame, nobility, intelligence, brightness, brilliance
Nabawiya	نبوية	prophetic

Nabiha	نبيهة	noble, famous, eminent, distinguished, brilliant, intelligent; fem. of Nabih
Nabila	نبيلة	noble, highborn, magnanimous, beautiful, intelligent, honourable; fem. of Nabil
Nida	نداء	call
Nadaa	ندى	dew, generosity, liberality, magnanimity
Nadi	ندىّ	moist, damp, tender, delicate
Nadia	ندّية	fem. of Nadi, dew, generosity, damp, tender, delicate
Nadida	نديدة	rival, equal
Nadima	نديمة	intimate friend, companion; fem. of Nadim نديم
Nadira	نادرة	rare, extraordinary, choice, precious; fem. of Nadir
Nadra	نضرة	radiance, bloom, glamour, brightness opulence, wealth
Nadwa	ندوة	council, club
Nafia	نافعة	profitable, beneficial, advantageous, useful, beneficial; fem. of Nafi
Nafisa	نفيسة	refined, pure, precious, delicate, choice, exquisite
Naghma	نغمة	melody, song
Nahar	نهار	day i.e. daytime
Shamsun Nahar	شمس النهار	sun of the day
Nahid	ناهيد	venus
Nahida	ناهيدة	fem. of Nahid ناهيد.
Nahiza	ناهضة	elevated, deligent
Nahla	نحلة	bee

Nahla	نهلة	a drink, a draught
Nail	نائل	winner, achiever, a boon, gift, acquirer
Naila	نائلة	fem. of Nail نائل.
Naima	نعيمة	happiness, peaceful, comfort, ease, pleasure, smooth, tender, bliss; fem. of Naim نعيم.
Najah	نجاح	success
Najat	نجات	safety, rescue, salvation, deliverance
Najiba	نجيبة	noble, excellent, generous, praiseworthy, distinguished, aristocratic
Najdah	نجدة	courage, bravery, help, succour
Najida	نجيدة	brave; a lady who accomplishes difficult tasks
Najia	ناجية	safe
Najiya	نجيَّة	intimate friend, bosom friend; fem. of Naji
Najla	نجلاء	large-eyed, wide-eyed
Najma	نجمة	star, a fine species of grass
Najmus Sahar	نجم السحر	the morning star
Najwa	نجوىٰ	confidential talk, secret conversation
Najwan	نجوان	saved, liberated
Nakhat	نكهت	fragrance
Nama	نعماء	gift, present, grace, favour, kindness
Naqiya	نقيّة	clear, pure, clean; fem. of Naqi
Naqa	نقاء	purity, refinement, clarity
Naqiba	نقيبة	mind, intellect, leader
Nargis (Per)	نرگس	narcissus (flower)
Narjis	نرجس	narcissus (flower)

Nasha	نشا	scent, perfume
Nashat	نشاط	liveliness, vigour, cheerfulness, joy, sprightliness, energy, vivacity
Nashita	نشيطة	energetic, dynamic, lively, fresh, vigorous
Nashwa	نشوىٰ	elated, exultant, flushed, enraptured; fem. of Nashwan
Nashwa	نشوة	fragrance, aroma
Nasiba	نسيبة	noble, highborn; fem. of Nasib
Nasila	نسيلة	honey that flows from the comb
Nasim	نسيم	breeze, gentle wind, fresh air, zephyr, fragrant air
Nasima	نسيمة	fem. of Nasim, zephyr, gentle wind
Nasira	نصيرة	helper, protector, friend, patron; fem. of Nasir
Nasrin	نسرين	Jonquil, Narcissus, wild rose, Jericho rose
Natiqa	ناطقة	one endowed with speech, eloquent, spokesperson; fem. of Natiq
Nawal	نوال	gift, present, grant, favour, grace, kindness
Nawar	نوار	flower, bud, blossom
Nawfa	نوفة	excess, surplus
Nawla	نولة	gift, present, grant, favour, grace
Nawra	نورة	blossom, flower
Nayyara	نيرة	luminous, shining; fem. of Nayyir
Nazaha	نزاهة	purity, righteousness, chastity, virtue, honesty
Nazanin (Per)	نازنين	elegant, delicate, beloved
Nazara	نضارة	bloom, beauty

Nazifa	نظيفة	pure, clean, neat, chaste, innocent; fem. of Nazif
Naziha	نزيهة	pure, virtuous, honest; fem. of Nazih
Nazira	نذيرة	warner, anything offered as a token of respect, anything given as sacrifice, a child who has been dedicated by his parents to serve Allah
Nazira	نظيرة	equal, like, alike, resembling, match, comparable; fem. of Nazir
Nazli	نظلى	delicate, feminine
Nibal	نبال	arrows
Nibras	نبراس	lamp
Nigar (Per)	نگار	picture, portrait, sweetheart
Nihel	نحل	presents, gifts
Nihla	نحلة	present, gift; sing. of Nihel نحل.
Nilufar (Per)	نيلوفر	water-lily
Nimat	نعمت	blessing, boon, favour, a gift from Allah, grace, bounty
Nimat	نعمات	blessings, boons, bounties; pl. of Nimat
Nisa	نساء	women
Qamarun Nisa	قمر النساء	moon of the women
Noshin	نوشين	sweet, pleasant, (i.e. dream)
Nuboogh	نبوغ	distinction, eminence, excellence, superiority
Nudra	ندرة	rarity, rareness. see Nadira نادرة.
Nudoora	ندورة	rareness
Nuha	نُهى	intelligence, intellect
Noor	نور	light, illumination
Noor Jahan	نور جهان	light of the world

Nooruddunya	نور الدنيا	light of the world
Noorun Nisa	نور النساء	light of the women
Noora	نورة	light; fem. of Noor
Nooraniyah	نورانية	luminous, brilliant
Nuriya	نوريّة	light, luminous, radiant, brilliant; fem. of Noori
Nusaiba	نسيبة	diminutive of Nasiba نسيبة, noble
Nusrat	نصرت	help, aid, assistance, support
Nuwwar	نوّار	pl. of Nuwwara نوّارة, blossom, flower
Nuwwara	نوارة	blossom, flower
Nuzar	نضار	pure gold
Nuzhat	نزهت	pleasure trip, freshness, promenade, excursion, recreation, cheerfulness

O

Obaida	عبيدة	See Ubayda
Ozza	عُزَّة	a baby fawn, young female deer, female fawn
Ola	علىٰ	See Ula
Orwiya	أروية	female mountain goat

P

Pari (Per)	پرى	fairy, fairy-like beautiful
Parsa (Per)	پارسا	chaste, devout, pious
Parvin	پروين	the Pleiades

Q

Qabila	قابلة	able, wise
Qadira	قادرة	powerful, able
Qahira	قاهرة	overpowering, victorious
Qamar	قمر	moon
Qamarun Nisa	قمر النساء	moon of the women
Qamra	قمراء	moonlight, moonlit, bright; fem. of Aqmar
Qasima	قاسمة	distributor, divider; fem. of Qasim
Qudsia	قدسية	holiness, sacredness, glorious, sacred, celestial, a blessed girl, a pious girl
Qurratulain	قرة العين	cooling or delight of the eye, joy, pleasure, darling, sweetheart

R

Rabia	رابعة	the fourth. ''*Rabia Basari*'', name of a saint who lived in Basrah
Rayia	راعية	guardian, custodian, patron, protector; fem. of Rayi
Raida	رائدة	explorer, guide, leader, pioneer, model, example; fem. of Raid
Raiqa	رائقة	pure, clear, tranquil, serene; fem. of Raiq
Rajia	راجية	hopeful, hoping, full of hope; fem. of Raji
Rajiha	راجحة	superior, predominant, fem. of Rajih
Rania	رانية	gazing

Rawia	راوية	narrator, reciter, transmitter (of ancient Arabic poetry)
Razia	راضية	satisfied, content, well-pleased; fem. of Razi
Rabab	رباب	usually two-stringed instrument
Rabia	ربيعة	spring, spring time, garden; fem. of Rabi.
Rabiha	رابحة	winner, gainer; fem. Rabih
Rabita	رابطة	band, bond, link, nexus
Rafat	رأفت	mercy, compassion, pity
Rafia	رفيعة	high ranking, noble, sublime, exquisite, exalted, eminent; fem. of Rafi
Rafida	رافدة	support, prop
Rafif	رفيف	glittering, shining, gleaming
Rafiqa	رفيقة	intimate friend, companion, associate; fem. of Rafiq
Rafraf	رفرف	cushion, eyeshade
Raghada	رغادة	comfort, opulence, affluence
Raghiba	راغبة	desirous, wishful, willing; fem. of Raghib
Raghd/Raghad	رَغد	pleasant, plenty
Raghid	رغيد	comfort, opulence, affluence, plenty
Rahat	راحة	rest, comfort, ease, relief
Rahifa	رهيفة	sharp; fem. of Rahif
Rahima	رحيمة	kind, compassionate; fem. of Rahim
Rahil	راحيل	wife of the Prophet Yaqub (Jacob). In the Bible she is mentioned as Rachel
Rahmat	رحمت	mercy, compassion, kindness

Raisa	رئيسة	leader, chief, princess, a noble lady, a wealthy lady
Rajab	رجب	the seventh month of the Islamic calendar
Rajiya	رجية	hope, expectation, wish
Rajwa	رجوىٰ	hope
Rakhima	رخيمة	soft, pleasant, melodious (voice)
Rakina	ركينة	firm, steady; fem. of Rakin ركين.
Ramazan/Ramadan	رمضان	the ninth month of the Islamic calendar
Ramla	رملة	sand. Wife of the Prophet Muhammadﷺ Her kunya is Umm Habiba
Rana	رنا	to gaze, look
Rana	رعناء	of elegant stature, soft, lovely, beautiful, graceful, delicate
Randa	رندة	scented, fragrant tree, good for decoration
Ranim	رنيم	singing, song, music
Raqia	راقية	superior, high ranking, educated; fem. of Raqi
Raqiba	رقيبة	guardian, supervisor
Raqiqa	رقيقة	delicate, fine, soft, slender, slim
Rasha	رشا	fawn, young gazelle
Rashaqa	رشاقة	graceful, stature, grace, elegance
Rasheeda	رشيدة	righteous, of good character, one who leads onto the right path
Rashida	راشدة	follower of the right path, mature, right minded, rightly guided; fem. of Rashid
Rashiqa	رشيقة	graceful, elegant; fem. of Rashiq

Rasikha	راسخة	well-established, well-founded, stable, steady; fem. of Rasikh
Rasima	راسمة	planner, designer; fem. of Rasim
Rasina	رصينة	calm, composed
Rasmiya	رسمِيَة	ceremonial, ceremonious, formal; fem. of Rasmi
Ratiba	راتبة	well-arranged, well-ordered
Raoom	رؤوم	loving, tender
Raunaq	رونق	beauty, grace, glamour, splendour
Raunaq Jahan (Ar. Per)	رونق جهان	lustre of the world
Raushan (Per)	روشن	light, luminous, bright, splendour
Raushan Ara (Per)	روشن آرا	adorning light (female)
Raushan Jabin (Per.Ar)	روشن جبين	of radiant forehead
Raushani (Per)	روشنى	light, splendour
Rawah	رواح	rest, repose
Rawza	روضة	garden
Raya	ريا	aroma, fragrance
Raihana	ريحانه	a handful of sweet basil. A bouquet of flowers; Wife of the Prophet Muhammad ﷺ
Razana	رزانة	calm, composure, self-possession
Razina	رزينة	calm, composed, self-possessed; fem. of Razin
Razia	رضيّة	delighted, satisfied, contended, pleased; fem. of Razi
Razwa	رضوىٰ	name of a moutain in Madina

Rifat	رفعت	dignity, exaltation, high rank, high standing
Rifqa	رفقة	kindness, gentleness, company, companionship. Wife of the Prophet Ishaq
Rifa	رفاء	happiness, prosperity
Rihab	رحاب	pl. of Rahbbah رحبة, vastness, expanse
Rim	ريم	white gazelle, antelope
Rima	ريمة	white gazelle, antelope
Riyaz	رياض	pl. of Rawza روضة, garden
Rizwan	رضوان	satisfaction, acceptance, pleasure, contentment, name of the gate-keeper of paradise
Rizwana	رضوانة	fem. of Rizwan. See Rizwan
Ruba	ربى	pl. of Rubwa, Rabwa ربوة, hill
Rubaba	ربابه	a two stringed musical instrument
Ruban	ربى	pl. of Rubwa ربوة, hill
Rubwa	ربوة	hill
Ruhaniya	روحانية	spirituality
Ruhiya	روحية	spiritual
Rakhshana	رخشانه	bright, brilliant, shining
Rumman	رمان	pl. of Rummana رمانة, pomegranate
Umm Rumman	ام رمان	mother of Ayesha (wife of the Prophet Muhammadﷺ)
Rummana	رمانة	pomegranate
Ruqa	روقة	pretty, beautiful
Ruqayya	رقيَّة	charming, attractive, captivating. Daughter of Muhammad (s), married to Khalifa Usman

Ruqya	رقية	charm, spell
Rushda	رشدیٰ	most rightly guided
Rushdiya	رشدية	rightly guided, on the right way, following the right path; fem. of Rushdi
Rua	رؤى	pl. of Ruya رؤيا, vision
Ruwaa	رواء	beauty, grace, prettiness, comeliness, pleasing appearance
Ruwaida	رُوَيدَا	walking gently
Ruya	رؤية	seeing, viewing, looking
Ruya	رؤيا	dream, vision

S

Sabiha	صابحة	coming or arriving in the morning; fem. of Sabih
Sabira	صابرة	patient, tolerant; fem. of sabir
Sadat	سعادت	happiness, bliss, felicity, success
Sadiqa	صادقة	true, truthful, honest, sincere, faithful, veracious, devoted; fem. of Sadiq
Safia	صافية	pure, clear, crystal; fem. of Saafi
Saiba	صائبة	straight, pertinent
Saida	صاعدة	rising, ascending; fem. of Said
Saida	ساعدة	branch, tributary
Saima	صائمة	fasting; fem. of Saim
Saliha	صالحة	pious, virtuous, just, a chaste woman, righteous
Salima	سالمة	safe, secure, perfect, sound, complete; fem. of Salim

Samia	سامية	eminent, exalted, lofty, elevated, high minded, sublime; fem. of Sami
Samira	ثامرة	fruit-bearing, fruitful, productive; fem. of Samir
Saba	سبا	queen saba, queen sheba
Saba	صبا	east wind
Sabah	صباح	morning, dawn
Sabaha	صباحة	beauty, gracefulness, handsomeness
Sabat	ثبات	firmness, stability, certainty, endurance, boldness, truth
Sabeera	صبيرة	patient, tolerant; fem. of Sabeer
Sabha	صبحى	pretty, beautiful, graceful, radiant; fem. of sabah صباح.
Sabia	سابية	captivating, enchanting, charming
Sabih	صبيح	pretty, beautiful, graceful
Sabiha	صبيحة	beautiful, handsome, morning
Sabiqa	سابقة	first, winner; fem. of Sabiq
Sabita	ثابتة	well established, certain, sure; fem. of Sabit
Sabriya	صبرية	patient; fem. of Sabri
Sabuh	صبوح	shining, brilliant
Sabura	صبورة	very patient, enduring
Sadida	سديدة	correct, right, sound, appropriate; fem. of Sadid
Sadiqa	صديقة	friend, companion; fem. of Sadiq
Sadiya	سعدية	happiness, luck, blissful, fortunate; fem. of Sadi
Sadooh	صدوح	singer, singing

Saduq	صدوق	honest, truthful, sincere, trustworthy
Saeeda	سعيدة	happy, lucky; fem. of Saeed
Safa	صفا	a hill near the sacred Kaaba; stone, rock
Safaa	صفاء	purity , clarity, serenity
Safiya	صفيّة	pure, righteous, untroubled, serene, the most valuable portions of the spoils of battle, sincere and honest friend; fem. of Safi صفى .
Safura	صافورا	wife of the Prophet Musa
Safwa	صفوة	the best part, elite, top, prime, flower
Saghira	صغيرة	small, slender, tender
Sahab	سحاب	clouds
Sahar	سحر	early dawn, early morning
Sahira	ساهرة	moon, a spring which flows constantly
Sahla	سهلة	smooth, simple, fluent, soft, facile, easy, even; fem. of Sahl
Sajida	ساجدة	prostrate in worship, bowing in adoration; fem. of Sajid
Sakha	سخاء	generosity, liberality
Sakhiya	سخيّة	generous, liberal, open handed
Sakina	سكينة	calmness, comfort, ease, tranquility, repose, serenity, peace of mind
Salam	سلام	peace, safety, security. See Salam (m.)
Salama	سلامة	peace, safety, security; fem. of Salamسلام.
Salma	سلمة	peace, fem. of Salm
Salima	سليمة	unhurt, affable, healthy, without defect, sound, perfect, complete, safe, secure; fem. of Salim

Salma	سلمیٰ	pacifist, peaceful
Salsabil	سلسبیل	a spring in Paradise
Salwa	سلویٰ	quail, solace
Salwah	سلوة	comfort, ease, amusement
Sama	سماء	heaven, sky
Samah	سماح	generosity, bounty, good-heartedness, large-heartedness
Saman	ثمن	price, value
Samar	سمر	pleasant conversation, evening or nightly conversation
Samiha	سمیحة	generous, kind, true, sincere, good-hearted, large-hearted, open- handed; fem. of Samih
Samim	صمیم	sincere, genuine, pure, true, essence, heart
Samima	صمیمة	true, sincere, genuine
Samina	سمینة	a healthy girl, fertile land without rock and stone.
Samina	ثمینة	valuable, costly, precious, priceless excellent; fem. of Smeen
Samira	سمیرة	companion (in nightly conversation), entertainer (with stories, music etc.) fem. of Samir
Samiqa	سامقة	lofty, towering
Sana	سناء	brilliance, radiance, resplendence, splendour, majestic
Sana	ثناء	praise, commendation, thankfulness, eulogy
Sanad	سند	support, prop, document
Saniya	سنیّة	brilliant, majestic, exalted, eminent, splendid; fem. of Sani

Sanjeeda	سنجيدة	weighted, guarded
Saqiba	ثاقبة	penetrating, piercing, sharp-witted, sagacious, acute; fem. of Saqib
Sara	ثراء	wealth
Sara	سارة	wife of the Prophet Ibrahim and mother of the Prophet Ismail
Sarab	سراب	mirage
Sarwa	ثروة	fortune, wealth, riches
Sausan, Susan	سوسن	lily of the valley, iris
Sawda	سودة	date-palm garden. Wife of the Prophet Muhammad ﷺ
Sayida	سيّدة	chief, leader, lady, Mrs; fem. of Sayyid
Sayidatun Nisa	سيّدة النساء	chief of woman
Shahida	شاهدة	witness; fem. of Shahid
Shaban	شعبان	the eighth month of the Islamic Calendar
Shabnam (Per)	شبنم	dew, a pendant of pearls
Shad (Per)	شاد	happy
Dilshad (Per)	دلشاد	of happy heart, happy, glad
Shadman (Per)	شادمان	glad, cheerful, joyful
Shadia	شادية	singer
Shadin	شادن	fawn, young deer
Shafaqat	شفقة	compassion, pity, kindness, tenderness
Shafia	شفيعة	mediatress; fem. of Shafi
Shafiqa	شفيقة	compassionate, kind-hearted, affectionate, tender, warm-hearted; fem. of Shafiq
Shahana (Per)	شاهانه	royal, kingly, splendid, magnificent
Shahida	شاهدة	witness, name of a sahabia (RA)

Shaheeda	شهيدة	martyr in the cause of Islam and as such held in very high esteem and honour; fem. of Shaheed شهيد
Shahin	شاهين	a royal white falcon, the beam of scales
Shahiqa	شاهقة	high, towering, lofty, tall; fem. of Shahiq
Shahira	شهيرة	famous, eminent, renowned; fem. of Shahir
Shahnaz (Per)	شهناز	a musical note, name of a melody
Shahrbanu (Per)	شهر بانو	lady of the city
Shahrin	شهر	month. Shahrin, the fully inflected form of Shahr appears in verse 3 of surat al-Qadr (no. 97)
Shahrzadah (Per)	شهرزاده	offspring of the city
Shahzadi (Per)	شاهزادى	princess
Shuaila	شعيلة	burning candle
Shaima	شيماء	daughter of Halima, the wet nurse of the Prophet Muhammadﷺ
Shaira	شاعرة	poetess, endowed with deep insight or intuition; fem. of Shair شاعر
Shajaratuddurr/ Shajratuddur	شجرة الدر	the tree of pearls, name of an Egyptian queen
Shajia	شجيعة	courageous, bold, brave; fem. of Shaji
Shakila	شكيلة	well formed, beautiful; fem. of Shakil
Shakira	شاكرة	thankful, grateful, contented; fem. of Shakir شاكر
Shakufa (Per)	شكوفة	blossom, opening bud
Shakura	شكورة	thankful, grateful; fem. of Shakur
Shamila	شاملة	complete, comprehensive
Shamail	شمائل	virtues; pl. of شميلة

Shama	شمعة	candle
Shamikh	شامخ	high, lofty, towering
Shamila	شميلة	natural disposition, character quality, virtue, a young shoot, a bud
Shamim	شميم	perfume, scent
Shamima	شميمة	sweet smell, flavour
Shahla	شهلاء	having grey eyes with a shade of red, a species of the narcissus flower
Shamma	شمه	pinch (of snuff)
Shams	شمس	sun
Shamsun Nahar	شمس النهار	sun of the day
Shamshad (Per)	شمشاد	tall and upright tree, box tree, graceful figure
Shamuda (Per)	شمودة	diamond
Shaqiqa	شقيقة	full sister
Shaqra	شقراء	blond, fair-haired, fair-complexioned; fem. of Ashqar اشقر.
Sharaf	شرف	nobility, high rank, eminence, distinction, honour
Sharifa	شريفة	noble, eminent, honourable, highborn; fem. of Sharif
Sharfa	شرفاء	most noble, gentle, urbane
Shaiba	شيبة	a variety of Artemisia
Shayma	شيماء	proper name. Daughter of Halima
Shaza	شذى	aroma, fragrance
Shazi	شذىّ	fragrant, aromatic
Sharmin (Per)	شرمن	shy, bashful, modest, coy

Shifa	شفاء	cure, healing, satsifaction, gratification
Shikoofa (Per.)	شگوفه	blossom
Shirin (Per)	شيرين	sweet, pleasant, gracious, delicate
Shuhrat	شهرت	fame, renown
Shukr	شكر	thanks, gratitude, gratefulness
Shuqra	شقراء	fair-complexioned, blonde
Shola	شعلة	flame, blaze
Siddiqa	صديقة	righteous, very truthful, honest; fem. of Siddiq
Sidra	سدرة	the "Lotus- tree at the farthest boundary" in paradise
Siham	سهام	arrows
Silma	سلمة	peace; fem. of Silm سلم.
Silmi	سلمى	peaceful
Simin (Per)	سيمين	silvery, made of Silver
Sitara	ستارة	veil, screen, curtain
Suad	سعاد	happiness, good fortune
Subaha	صباحة	beautiful, graceful
Subh	صبح	dawn, aurora, morning
Sufiya	صوفية	a mystic, someone believing in Sufi mysticism; fem. of Sufi
Sughra	صغرى	small, slender, tender
Suha	سها	"dim star in Ursa Minor"
Suhaila	سهيل	canopus
Suhaima	سهيمة	small arrow
Suhair	سهير	proper name

Sukaina	سكينة	diminutive of Sakina سكينة, calmness
Sulaima	سليمى	diminutive of Salma سلمى, beloved
Sultana	سلطانة	queen, woman ruler, wife of a Sultan; fem. of Sultan
Sulafa	سلافة	choicest, (wine)
Sulwa	سلوة	comfort, ease, amusement, solace
Sumaya	سمية	diminutive of Samia سامية, high
Sunbula	سنبلة	ear of corn
Sundus	سندس	silk brocade
Surayya	ثريّا،ثرية	the Pleiades, clustre of seven brilliant stars in taurus, a wealthy lady, lustre, chandelier
Susan	سوسن	lily of the valley, iris

T

Tabassum	تبسم	smile, happiness
Taghrid	تغريد	singing, cooing
Tahani	تهانى	pl. of Tahniat تهنئة, congratulation, felicitation, well-wishing
Tahira	طاهرة	chaste, pure, pious, clean; fem. of Tahir
Tahiya	تحية	greeting, salutation, cheer, welcome
Tahmina (Per)	تهمينة	wife of the famous persian hero Rustam and mother of Sohrab
Tahseen	تحسين	adornment, ornament, decoration, embellishment, betterment, praise, beautification
Taiba	تائبة	one who refrains from evil-doings; repentant; fem. of Ta'ib تائب

Taif	طيف	vision, spectre
Taj	تاج	crown
Taliba	طالبة	student, seeker, pursuer; fem. of Talib
Tamanna	تمنّى	to wish, to desire, to hope
Tamanni	تمنّى	wish, wishing (for), desire
Tamazur	تماضر	brilliant, whiteness
Tanjia	تنجية	rescue, salvation, deliverance
Tanweer	تنوير	illuminating, lighting
Tanzila	تنزيلة	revelation, sending down; fem. of Tanzil
Taqiya	تقيّة	Godfearing, devout, pious; fem. of Taqi
Trana (Per)	ترانه	melody, song
Tarib	طرب	lively, geeful, merry
Tarifa	طريفة	rare, exquisite thing or object
Taroob	طروب	lively, gleeful, merry
Tasiyah	تأسية	consolation, comfort
Taslima	تسليمة	greeting, salutation; fem. of Taslim
Tasnim	تسنيم	a spring in paradise
Tawfiqa	توفيقة	prosperity, good luck, good-fortune, success (granted by Allah); fem. of Tawfiq
Tawaddud	تودد	endearment, showing love or affection to, gaining the love of another
Tiba	طيبة	goodness, good nature
Taisir	تيسير	felicitation
Tayyiba	طيّبة	good, good-natured, sweet, agreeable, generous, good-tempered; fem. of Tayyib
Tayyibatun Nisa	طيبة النساء	good-natured (one) of the women

Tazima	تعظيمة	glorification, exaltation, honour; fem. of Tazim
Tuhfa	تحفة	gift, present
Turfa	طرفة	rarity, rare object, novelty

U

Ubayda	عبيدة	female servant of lower rank; fem. of Ubayd
Ula	علىٰ	high rank, prestige, glory
Ulfat	ألفت	friendship, intimacy, love, attachment
Ulya	عليا	higher, highest; fem. of Ala اعلى
Umama	أمامة	proper name. Name of grand daughter of the Prophet Muhammadﷺ
Umayma	أميمة	diminutive of Umm أمّ, mother
Umm	امّ	mother. Used as an attributive, to make a compound of which the first part is Umm
Umm Ayman	أم ايمن	mother of the blessed
Umm Fazl	أم فضل	mother of favour, bounty
Umm Habiba	أم حبيبة	Wife of the Prophet Muhammadﷺ. Her name is Ramla; Umm Habiba is her Kunya (nickname) after the name of her daughter Habiba
Umm Hani	أم هانى	name of the daughter of Abu Talib and sister of Ali (RA)
Umm Kulsum	أم كلثوم	daughter of the Prophet Muhammadﷺ, married to Khalifa Usman (uthman) after the death of her sister Ruqayya

Umm Slama	أم سلمة	Wife of Muhammadﷺ. Her name was Hind
Umm Salma	أم سلمى	name of the beloved mother of first khalifa Abu Bakr (RA)
Umm Rooman	أم رومان	name of the sacred wife of first Khalifa Abu Bakr (RA) mother of Hazrat Ayesha (RA)
Ummid (Per)	أميد	hope
Umniya	أمنية	wish, desire, hope
Unquda	عنقودة	bunch of grapes
Urwa	عروة	support, handhold. Description of Ayesha by Muhammadﷺ
Uzma	عظمى	greatest, more magnificent, more glorious; fem. of Azam أعظم

W

Warisa	وارثة	heiress
Wasiqa	واثقة	confident, sure, certain; fem. of Wasiq
Wafiqa	وافقة	successful
Wadad	وداد	love, friendship
Wadi	وديع	gentle, calm
Waddia	ودية	amicable, friendly
Wadida	وديدة	attached, devoted, friendly, fond
Wafa	وفاء	faithfulness, fidelity, loyalty, faith
Wafia	وافية	faithful, loyal
Wafiqa	وفيقة	successful; fem. of Wafiq

Wafiya	وفيَّة	true, trustworthy, reliable, loyal, faithful, perfect, complete; fem. of Wafi
Wahiba	واهبة	giver
Wahida	وحيدة	one, exclusive, unique, matchless, singular; fem. of Wahid
Wajida	واجدة	achiever, excited, finder, lover; fem. of Wajid
Wajiha	وجيهة	high, eminent, distinguished, honoured, well-esteemed, illustrious; fem. of Wajih
Wallada	ولادة	prolific, fertile, fruitful
Walidah	وليدة	newborn child
Waliyah	ولية	friend
Wardah	وردة	rose, deep red colour
Wasama	وسامة	beauty, gracefulness, prettiness
Wasila	وصيلة	inseparable friend
Wasima	وسيمة	beautiful, pretty, graceful, handsome of face, goodly, elegant; fem. of Wasim
Wasma	وسماء	a pretty face, beautiful, graceful
Widad	وداد	love, friendship
Wijdan	وجدان	ecstasy, sentiment
Wisal	وصال	communion in love
Wisam	وسام	decoration, medal, badge of honour

Y

Yakta (Per)	يكتا	unique, incomparable
Yaqoot	ياقوت	ruby, sapphire, topaz
Yasim	ياسم	jasmine

Yasmin	يسمين،ياسمين	the flower called jasmine
Yumna	يمنة	happiness, success; fem. of Yumn يمن.
Yusra	يسرىٰ	left-hand side, state of ease
Yumna	يمنىٰ	right-hand, right, fortunate, lucky, blessed; fem. of Ayman أيمن.

Z

Zahira	زاهرة	bright, brilliant, shining, luminous, distinguished, lofty
Zaida	زائدة	increasing, exceeding, excessive, growing, surplus; fem. of Zaid
Zabya	ظبية	female gazelle
Zafira	ظافرة	victorious, triumphant, successful, winner, conqueror; fem. of Zafir
Zaghlula	زغلولة	young pigeon; fem. of Zaghlul
Zahabia	ذهبية	golden, precious
Zahia	زاهية	beautiful, brilliant, glowing; fem. of Zahi
Zahida	زاهدة	devout, ascetic, a hermit, self-denying
Zahira	ظهيرة	helper, supporter, protector, patron; fem. of Zahir
Zahra	زهراء	bright, brilliant, radiant, shining, luminous; fem. of Azhar أزهر.
Zahrah	زهرة	flower, blossom, beauty
Zaib (Per)	زَيب	beauty
Zaima	زعيمة	leader
Zahratun Nisa	زهرة النساء	flower of women

Zakira	ذاكرة	one who glorifies or eulogises Allah; fem. of Zakir
Zakiya	زكيّة	pure, chaste, sinless, fem. of Zakiy زكيّ.
Zakiya	ذكية	intelligent, bright, brilliant, sharp-witted.
Zarifa	ظريفة	elegant, witty, graceful; fem. of Zarif
Zarin (Per)	زرين	golden
Zarina (Per)	زرينة	golden
Zarqa	زرقاء	bluish green (eyes)
Zayna	زينة	fem. of Zayn: embellishment, adornment, decoration, ornament
Zaynab	زينب	name of a beautiful tree exuding fragrance. Names of two wives and one daughter of the Prophet Muhammadﷺ and one daughter of Khalifa Ali
Zaitun	زيتون	the olive tree or the olive fruit
Zaytuna	زيتونة	olive; fem. of Zaytun زيتون.
Zeb Ara (Per)	زيب آرا	adorning ornament
Zebun Nisa	زيب النساء	adornment of women
Zeba	زيبا	pretty, beautiful
Ziba	ظباء	pl. of Zaby ظبى, gazelle
Zinat	زينت	adornment, ornament, decoration, elegance, beauty
Zinatun Nisa	زينت النساء	ornament of women
Zinat	زينات	pl. of Zinat زينة, ornament
Ziyada	زيادة	increase, addition, surplus, superabundance
Ziyan	زيان	ornament, decoration

Zuha	ضحى	brightness, early morning
Zubaida	زبيدة	diminutive of Zubda زبدة, butter, cream. Elite, choicest part, quintessence, essence, prime, flower
Zuhaira	زهيرة	floret, small flower
Zuhra	زهرة	venus, brilliancy, brightness, flower
Zuhur	زهور	pl. of Zahrah زهرة, flower
Zulaikha	زليخا	wife of the king of Egypt (Pharaonic age) who was attracted by the beauty of the Prophet Yusuf/Joseph
Zulfa	زلفاء	having a small and finely chiselled nose
Zurafa	ظرفاء	elegant, witty, graceful; fem. of Zarif ظريف.

Names of Historical Importance

The Companions (Sahaba)

Abbas ibn Mirdas	عباس ابن مرداس
Abdullah ibn Umar	عبد الله ابن عمر
Abdullah ibn Abbas	عبد الله ابن عباس
Abdullah ibn Zaid	عبد الله ابن زيد
Abdullah ibn Zubair	عبد الله ابن زبير
Abu Barza ibn Abdullah	أبو برزة ابن عبدالله
Abu Huraira ibn Amir	ابو هريرة ابن عامر
Abu Jandal	أبو جندل
Abul Aas	أبو العاص
Abu Musa Ashari ibn Amir	أبو موسىٰ اشعرى ابن عامر
Abu Ubaida ibn Jarrah	أبو عبيده ابن جراح
Abu Zar Ghifari ibn Junada	أبوذر غفارى ابن جنادة
Amir ibn Rabiah	عامر ابن ربيعة
Ammar ibn Yasir	عمار ابن ياسر
Ali ibn Abi Talib	على ابن أبى طالب
Bilal ibn Ribah	بلال ابن رباح
Hamzah ibn Abdul Muttalib	حمزة ابن عبد المطلب
Harith ibn Hisham	حارث ابن هشام
Hasan ibn Ali	حسن ابن على
Hassan ibn Thabit	حسن ابن ثابت
Huzaifa ibn Al-Yaman	حذيفة ابن اليمان

Jafar ibn Abi Talib	جعفر ابن أبى طالب
Jabir ibn Abdullah	جابر ابن عبدالله
Khalid ibn Waleed	خالد ابن وليد
Muaz ibn Jabal	معاذ ابن جبل
Muawiah ibn Abi Sufyan	معاوية ابن ابى سفيان
Mughira ibn Shoba	مغيرة ابن شعبة
Musab ibn Umair	مصعب ابن عمير
Noman ibn Bashir	نعمان ابن بشير
Qatada ibn Noman	قتادة ابن نعمان
Rafaah ibn Rafe	رفاعة ابن رافع
Saad ibn Abi Waqqas	سعد ابن أبى وقاص
Saad ibn Ubada	سعد ابن عبادة
Saeed ibn Al-Aas	سعيد ابن العاص
Saeed ibn Amir	سعيد ابن عامر
Salman Farsi	سلمان فارسى
Suhaib ibn Sinan	صهيب ابن سنان
Safwan ibn Umayyah	صفوان ابن أمية
Talha ibn Abdullah	طلحة ابن عبد الله
Urvah ibn Masood	عروة ابن مسعود
Uthman ibn Affan	عثمان ابن عفان
Umar ibn Al-Khattab	عمر ابن الخطاب
Waqid ibn Abdullah	واقد ابن عبد الله
Yazeed ibn Abi Sufyan	يزيد ابن أبى سفيان
Yasar (the slave of the Prophet Muhammad)	يسار (مولى رسول الله)
Zabraqan ibn Badr	زبرقان ابن بدر
Zaid ibn Thabit	زيد ابن ثابت

Zakwan ibn Jundub	ذكوان ابن جندب
Ziyad ibn Labid	زياد ابن لبيد
Zubair ibn Abdulah	زبير ابن عبد الله

The Female Companions (Sahabiyat)

Ayesha Al-Siddiqa	عائشة الصديقة
Anisa bint Adi	أنيسة بنت عدى
Asma bint Abi Bakr	أسماء بنت أبى بكر
Aaminah bint Ruqaish	آمنة بنت رقيش
Barirah bint Muhammad	بريرة بنت محمد
Fatima Al-Zahra	فاطمة الزهراء
Fidhdha	فضة
Fukaiha bint Yasar	فكيهة بنت يسار
Habibah bint Abdullah	حبيبة بنت عبد الله
Hafsa bint Umar	حفصة بنت عمر
Hamamah	حمامة
Hasanah	حسنة
Haula bint Tuwait	حولاء بنت تويط
Hauva bint Yazeed	حوا بنت يزيد
Hind bint Utba	هند بنت عتبة
Jamila bint Saad	جميلة بنت سعد
Jamanah bint Abu Talib	جمانة بنت أبى طالب
Juwairiah bint Harith	جويرية بنت حارث
Khalidah bint Harith	خالدة بنت حارث
Khansh bint Amr	خنساء بنت عمرو
Khaulah bint Hakam	خولة بنت حكم
Khdijatul Kubra	خديجة الكبرىٰ

Lubana bint Sawar	لبانة بنت سوار
Maimunah bint Harith	ميمونة بنت حارث
Mariya Qibtia	مارية قبطية
Mulaikah bint Malik	مليكة بنت مالك
Raihanah bint Shamoon	ريحانة بنت شمعون
Ruqayyah bint Muhammadﷺ	رقية بنت محمد
Safiyyah bint Haee	صفية بنت حيى
Salamah bint Hurr	سلامة بنت حر
Salma bint Umais	سلمى بنت عميس
Saudah bint Zama	سودة بنت زمعة
Suhailah bint Masood	سهيلة بنت مسعود
Sumayyah bint Khayyat	سمية بنت خياط
Tayyiba bint Wahab	طيبة بنت وهب
Um Ammarah bint Nasiba bint kaab	أم عمارة بنت نسيبة بنت كعب
Um Habibah bint Abi Sufian	أم حبيبة بنت ابى سفيان
Um Hani bint Abi Talib	أم هانى بنت ابى طالب
Um Kulthoom bint Muhammadﷺ	أم كلثوم بنت محمد
Ummul Khair bint Sakhr	أم الخير بنت صخر
Um Ralah	أم رعلة
Um Rooman bint Amir	أم رومان بنت عامر
Um Salama bint Abi Umayyah	أم سلمة بنت ابى امية
Zainab bint Khuzaimah	زينب بنت خزيمة

Successors to the Companions (Tabi'un)

Abu Idrees	أبو ادريس
Abu Ishaq	أبو اسحاق

Abu Salmah ibn Sahl	أبو سلمة ابن سهل
Abu Uthman ibn Sannad Al-Khuzaee	أبو عثمان ابن سند الخزاعى
Ahnaf	أحنف
Alqamah ibn Qais	عقمة ابن قيس
Amir ibn Salih	عامر ابن صالح
Aswad	أسود
Ata ibn Yazeed	عطاء ابن يزيد
Uwais ibn Amir	أويس ابن عامر
Ayyub ibn Al-Bukhari Al-Yamani	أيوب ابن البخارى اليمانى
Hakam	حكم
Harim	هرم
Ibrahim ibn Muhammad	إبراهيم ابن محمد
Jabir	جابر
Khalid ibn Usaid	خالد ابن اسيد
Makhool	مكحول
Mus'ir	مسعر
Nafie	نافع
Qatadah ibn Rabi	قتادة ابن ربيع
Qubaisah ibn Jabir	قبيصة ابن جابر
Rabie	ربيع
Safwan	صفوان
Salim	سالم
Shuraih	شريح
Thabit ibn Qatba	ثابت ابن قطبة
Wahb ibn Ajwa	وهب ابن اجوع
Yunus	يونس

Commentators on the Quran (Mufassirun)

Abdullah	عبد الله
Abu Abdullah	أبو عبد الله
Abu Hayyan	أبو حيان
Abul Aliyah	أبو العالية
Ali ibn Abi Talib	علي ابن أبي طالب
Ayyub	أيوب
Habib	حبيب
Hasan	حسن
Ibn Majah	إابن ماجه
Ikramah	عكرمة
Ismaeel	إسماعيل
Mahmood	محمود
Mansoor	منصور
Mujahid	مجاهد
Muslim	مسلم
Ubai	أبي
Qatadah	قتاده
Saeed	سعيد
Shahabuddin	شهاب الدين
Shoba	شعبة
Sufyan	سفيان
Taoos	طاؤس
Wakee	وكيع

Scholars of Hadith (Muhaddisun)

Abdul-Baqi	عبد الباقى
Abdul Haque	عبد الحق
Abdullah	عبد الله
Abdur-Razzaque	عبدالرزاق
Abu Abdullah	أبو عبد الله
Abu Awana	أبو عوانة
Abu Bakr	أبو بكر
Abu Daood	ابو داؤد
Abu Jafar	أبو جعفر
Abul Hasan	أبو الحسن
Abul Qasim	أبو القاسم
Abu Muhammad	أبو محمد
Abu Naeem	أبو نعيم
Ahmad	أحمد
Ishaque	إسحاق
Iyadh	عياض
Jamaluddin	جمال الدين
Malik	مالك
Muhammad ibn Ismaeel Al-Bukhari	محمد ابن إسماعيل البخارى
Muslim	مسلم
Noorul Haque	نور الحق
Noorul Islam	نور الاسلام
Saeed	سعيد
Shaikh Ali	شيخ على

Salamullah	سلام الله
Sherwaih	شيرويه
Waliuddin	ولى الدين
Yahya	يحىٰ

Muslim Jurists (Fuqaha)

Abu Bakr ibn Abdur Rahman	أبو بكر ابن عبد الرحمٰن
Abu Hanifa (Numan ibn Thabit)	أبو حنيفة (نعمان ابن ثابت)
Abu Salma	أبو سلمه
Ahmad	أحمد
Azzuddin	عز الدين
Ibn Hazm, Jafar	إبن حزم جعفر
Kharija	خارجة
Laith	ليث
Ubaidullah ibn Abbas	عبيد الله عباس
Qasim	قاسم
Saeed ibn Al-Aas	سعيد ابن العاص
Salim (slave of Abu Huzaifa)	سالم مولىٰ أبى حذيفة
Sulaiman ibn Sarw	سليمان ابن صرر
Shafei (Muhammad)	شافعى (محمد)
Urwah ibn Masood Al-Saqfi	عروة ابن مسعود الثقفى
Zaid ibn Thabit	زيد ابن ثابت

THE HOLY
QUR'AN

ABDULLAH YUSUF ALI

PRESENTING
THE QUR'AN

A BRIEF INTRODUCTION TO ALL THE
114 CHAPTERS OF THE QUR'AN

SANIULLAH KHAN

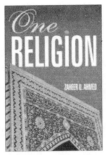

One
RELIGION

ZAHEER U. AHMED

The
Alhambra

Washington Irving

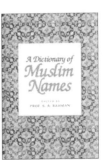

A Dictionary of
Muslim
Names

EDITED BY
PROF. S. A. RAHMAN

The Travels of
Ibn Battúta

H.A.R. GIBB

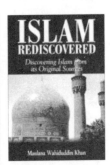

ISLAM
REDISCOVERED

Discovering Islam from
its Original Sources

Maulana Wahiduddin Khan

THE
SPREAD
OF
ISLAM
IN THE WORLD

A History of Peaceful Preaching

Prof. Thomas Arnold

The Travels of
Ibn Jubayr

Roland Broadhurst

Humayun
Nama

The History of Humayun

Gul-Badan Begam

A HISTORY OF
ARABIAN MUSIC

HENRY GEORGE FARMER

THE
Quran
FOR
Astronomy
AND
Earth Exploration from Space

S. Waqar Ahmed Husaini

A Literary
History of Persia
Edward G. Browne
VOLUMES I & II

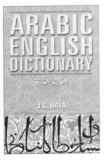

ARABIC
ENGLISH
DICTIONARY

J. G. HAVA

The Beautiful
Commands of
ALLAH

THE MORISCOS OF
SPAIN

HENRY CHARLES LEA

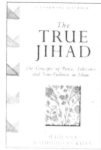
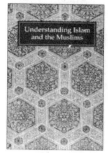

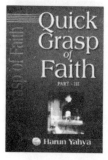
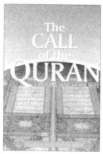

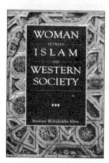
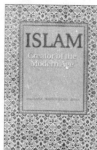

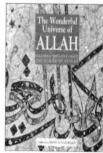